POSITIVE CLASSROOM MANAGEMENT

by Terri Breeden
and Emalie Egan

Incentive Publications, Inc.
Nashville, Tennessee

Illustrated by Gayle Harvey
Cover design and illustration by Bill Latta
Edited by Anna Quinn

Library of Congress Catalog Card Number: 96-78572
ISBN 0-86530-355-x

PRINTED IN THE UNITED STATES OF AMERICA

Table of Contents

ABOUT THIS BOOK

Positive Classroom Management was written with the belief that the goal of discipline is self-discipline and on the premise that students can be taught to control their own behavior. Words and ideas are powerful tools for solving problems. These activities and routines were developed to show that universal values can be applied in classrooms to elevate the dialogue about how reasonable people should behave.

The words and ideas contained in this book reflect a positive, proactive approach to dealing with common (and not so common) classroom behavior issues. The strategies focus on preventive methods rather than punitive actions. When problems arise in the classroom, count to ten and then grab this book! It will allow you to see alternative solutions and strategies that will expand your management repertoire. Some ideas should be reserved for times when severe and dramatic measures must be taken, while others are potent preventive medicine. Don't give up on yourself or your students . . . take action!

Use your strengths. Browse through this book and select the ideas that are compatible with your personal style. If one of your strengths is the love of your subject matter, then plan interventions that reinforce learning. If one of your strengths is structure, then organize your learning environment to promote positive behavior. If one of your strengths is humor, then break loose and have fun. Remember that this is not a step-by-step foolproof manual, rather, it is a cornucopia of positive management tools to help you control and enliven your classroom environment.

For the very true beginning of her wisdom is the desire of discipline; and the care of discipline is love.

–from The Apocrypha

The Tone of the Setting . . .
Celebrations, Rituals, & Rules

THE TEACHER'S MISSION STATEMENT

When starting a business, the first item on the agenda is to create a mission statement for the organization. The mission statement gives a focus to all other aspects of the company. Before the business embarks on new initiatives, the company's officials determine if the new idea is in line with the mission statement. The mission statement sets the direction for the company.

Teachers need to create their own mission statements. Most school systems have one that guides the school system as a whole. That statement is a good place to begin when writing a teacher's mission statement. For example, one school system's statement is as follows:

> *To ensure that all students are empowered with the knowledge, the skills, and the character to become: lifelong learners; successful, productive workers; and caring, global citizens; who practice and extend democratic principles.*
>
> (Metropolitan Nashville Public Schools, 1994)

From this broad mission statement, a teacher can define the specific part he or she will emphasize to the students in the school system. For example, if a social studies teacher was writing his or her mission statement, the focus could be on "creating global citizens who practice and extend democratic principles."

At times, mission statements tend to contain broad phrases that do not touch the individual. It is critical that a teacher's mission statement be relevant to him or her. The following questions will serve as a guide for you as you develop your own mission statement:

- What skills are essential for my students' futures?
- What should be valued by my students?
- If I met my students as adults, what would I want to hear that they had accomplished?
- If my students were writing my epitaph, what would I want them to say about me?

Reflect on these questions and then write your mission statement below.

Your mission statement: _____

_____

_____

_____

_____

_____

_____

_____

_____

GIVING STUDENTS OWNERSHIP OF THE CLASSROOM ROUTINES

Classroom Constitution

When students share responsibility for the development of the rules and expectations that guide classroom activities, they are far more likely to understand the necessary limits on their behavior. Additionally, they are committed to showing respect for expectations. There are many ways to encourage participation in the development of classroom rules. Holding a constitutional convention and creating a classroom constitution give your class an opportunity to celebrate the accomplishment as a group.

Read the Preamble to the Constitution of the United States to the students.

> *We the People of the United States, in order to form a more perfect Union, establish Justice, insure domestic Tranquility, provide for the common defense, promote the general Welfare, and secure the Blessings of Liberty to ourselves and our Posterity, do . . .*

You could say the following to the students:

> *Our country has a mission to insure the best possible life for everyone in our country. The Constitution begins by explaining that mission. The Constitution lays out laws and rules to make life as fair as possible for all people. (Explain that the school system has a mission and has rules based on that mission.) The system has responsibilities to the community, so there are rules and limits that everyone in the system must observe. We will now write a mission statement for our class. This mission statement will help us later when we write our class constitution. Think for a few minutes of all the things that are important so that our class can be successful, peaceful, and happy. We will listen to everyone's ideas and combine them into a mission statement for our class.*

Young children will need help combining the statements, but older students may elect a committee to work on the wording of the mission statement. When the mission of the class has been established, read the mission statement (Preamble) to the class.

An appropriate comment for you to make at this point could be the following:

> *Our mission statement adds to the mission statements of our school and our school system. Now that we have a mission statement, we know what we are about and why we are here. Think for a minute about the rules we need to accomplish this. Let's make some suggestions.*

Ask the students to make suggestions for classroom rules and expectations and combine these into the constitution. Ask the students to verify that the constitution matches the mission statement.

When the constitution has been debated and written, call for a Constitutional Convention. Cut a large piece of brown craft paper in the shape of a scroll. Ask students to write the rules on the constitution in large letters. Decorate the document with glitter and a gold paint pen. Post the document in a prominent location where it may be reviewed often. At the convention, invite an inspiring administrator to give words of encouragement and reflection. The custodians and cafeteria workers may be honored guests. Students are invited to stand and ratify the constitution by voice vote.

To add a bit more ceremony to the convention, print the class pledge on small sheets of paper and tape it to the pens that the students will use to sign the document. Students may elect to dress up on this momentous occasion. Students stand and repeat the pledge to uphold the constitution of the class.

I, _____ , as a member of

this class, as a member of the _____ team,

and as a student at _____ School

do hereby pledge to uphold the constitution of our class to

the best of my ability, to respect the rights of others in our

class, and to encourage others to uphold the constitution.

Before the signing ceremony, tell students about the signing of the Declaration of Independence. You could say the following:

> *The original signers of the Constitution became wanted men and signed the historic words on pain of death. When John Hancock signed the Declaration of Independence, he used large letters and a flourishing penmanship style because he said that he wanted King George to be able to read it without his spectacles. It is tempting today to sign this important document as John Hancock did, but there will be only room to sign in the usual manner. Bring your pen to the constitution as you are called, and after you sign, you may return to your seat and keep the pen.*

(You may want to include lines for the students' signatures.) Each student then signs the constitution and keeps the pen. You may choose to serve simple refreshments to mark the occasion. Patriotic music is an appropriate backdrop.

Periodically review the constitution and remind students of their commitment to uphold it. It may be necessary to remind some students often in private conversations. It is important to emphasize that the constitution is the document that guides the class and that everyone must comply with the rules as they have promised.

PREVENTION

If a teacher puts energy into prevention, the students will reap the benefits! There is no punishment after misbehavior that has the impact of gentle prevention before improper behavior can occur. The checklist below will increase a faculty's awareness of preventive measures.

- Teachers concentrate on creating a warm, friendly, businesslike atmosphere.
- Students have an opening routine that is followed every day, such as Chart Work. (See page 26.)
- Teachers build rapport with their students.
- Teachers call parents and introduce themselves before problems arise.
- Teachers stand at their doors during transitions.
- Teachers remain near their students during assemblies.
- Teachers model attentive behavior at assemblies and during announcements.
- Rules are clearly posted.
- Teachers make sure students are settled in the cafeteria before leaving.
- Teachers have a plan for monitoring students when they must be out of the room.
- The school has convenient phones permitting teachers to call parents.
- Parents are warmly welcomed into the school.
- Problems on the bus or at the bus stop are resolved early in the day.
- Students have access to cooling off places where they are safe and monitored.
- Teachers have a plan for handling serious disruption.
- Graffiti is removed immediately.
- Students have assigned seats.
- Substitute teachers have emergency plans, seating charts, and class rolls.
- Teachers closely support substitute teachers.
- Students have written hall passes before they leave the room.
- Parents and students are aware of consequences for misbehavior.
- Teachers have access to assignment sheets, checklists, and clipboards.
- Teachers have suggestion boxes handy for students to leave anonymous notes.
- Students are carefully supervised before and after school.
- Distractions are minimized.
- Irresistible hazards are removed.
- The students' days are paced with a variety of planned activities.
- Teachers have a bag of tricks for unavoidable delays and unplanned glitches.
- Students recognize cues for being quiet and taking their seats.
- The school system has a no tolerance policy that addresses drugs, weapons, and assault.
- The school has distributed a student handbook to students and their parents.

DOCUMENTATION

A student who has a chronic problem with behavior requires careful monitoring. By documenting behaviors and describing strategies that are successful, teachers will discover means of assisting students with behavior problems. As any good scientist knows, it is also important to record strategies that have proven unsuccessful. By making notes on each incident, describing the surrounding events, and evaluating the effectiveness of the intervention, teachers create a valuable source of information.

This documentation may hold any of the following material:
- copies of letters to parents
- three-part forms (See page 60.)
- anecdotal cards (See page 59.)
- samples of Designs for Improvement (See page 126.)
- notes from the Dreaded Clipboard (See page 72.)
- anecdotal evidence
- notes from parents
- notes from telephone conversations

Vital elements of documentation:
- maintain confidentiality
- date all materials
- file documentation as quickly as possible
- look for patterns of behavior

Administrators appreciate having a well-documented file when they have to take strong action. The dates and notes in the file protect you and the administration in the event the decisions are challenged. Parents also appreciate having an accurate picture of the student's behavior. Often students are not aware of the magnitude of their problems until they see them in black and white. The power of the printed word should not be underestimated.

WHEN COUNTING TO TEN FAILS

No matter how much a teacher enjoys students, there is no doubt every teacher at some time loses his or her patience. When the normal strategies for regaining self-control fail, try one (or two or three) of the suggestions below:

1. **Remember who is the adult and who is the child.** When a student has "pushed your buttons," it is not uncommon to react without remembering that you are dealing with a child. Middle grade students can upset a person as much, if not more, than an adult. Allow professional behavior to overrule an emotional response. Stop and remember that as the adult in the situation there are guidelines that must be followed and allowing one's emotions to dictate the response is unacceptable.

2. **Give yourself some space.** When a situation arises that doesn't have an easy solution, inform the student that at the moment it is impossible to decide on what the appropriate punishment should be for the offense. Explain to the student that what he or she has done is very disturbing and more time will be needed before a solution can be found. This is a very powerful intervention. This strategy allows you to distance yourself from the situation. Tempers can cool and advice can be sought. This strategy also worries the student. He or she usually has some time to reflect on the situation during this cool-down time. Generally, this allows the student to see the situation from a slightly different perspective. A student will be worried about what the punishment will be. This often makes the student easier to deal with when the punishment is given.

3. **Ignore the student.** There are many things going on in a classroom that you can not and should not ignore. Yet, ignoring is very appropriate when you feel that the bad behavior is occurring because the student is only seeking attention. If the student, for example, is loudly tapping a pencil on the desk, ignore it. Look around the classroom and find someone who is acting appropriately and verbally praise that student. It is also critical to watch the student who was tapping the pencil and try to find a positive behavior that he or she *is* doing. Praise the appropriate behavior. In the end, the student will learn that attention comes from appropriate behavior—not inappropriate behavior.

4. **Don't get angry . . . take action.** Middle school students are experts at exasperating adults. Don't let them win. Develop effective strategies for inappropriate behaviors and use them. Don't threaten. Don't nag. Take action. If the rule states that a certain behavior will result in a phone call to the parents, call the parents. If you stated that if an assignment is late it will have five points deducted, deduct five points. Don't waste time and energy dealing with behavior that has already been addressed in the class rules or in the student handbook.

5. **Get some rest.** When a person is tired, he or she cannot be at their best. If you find that all the students are aggravating you, you are probably tired. No matter how many papers need grading, no matter how much the bulletin board needs changing, leave school on time, go home, and get some rest. Teaching is a very emotionally draining career. Rest is critical to be the best teacher you can be.

6. **Keep a sense of humor.** Children are fun, forgiving, and playful. They need to feel accepted by their teachers. Laugh with them and feel free to laugh at yourself. Mrs. Smith told of an incident in her classroom where a bad fight broke out between two large, strong eighth-grade boys. One boy was pounding the other boy's head into the heater. The 120-pound teacher had to do something to break up the fight. She grabbed the arm of the boy who was hitting the other boy. Loudly and quickly she jumped up and down and told him to STOP. He stopped, probably because of the ruckus the teacher was making. The boys were taken to the office and the teacher, worn and shaken, returned to the classroom. As the incident was being discussed by the class before the teacher resumed teaching, one student remarked, "Ms. Smith, you sure looked silly jumping up and down and grabbing that boy's arm." After all the tension caused by the fight, the teacher just cracked up and told the class that she just wasn't thinking about how silly she had looked at the time. She mentioned that she would try to not look so silly next time. Laughter is still good medicine.

7. **Realize that you are not alone.** Teachers need the support of other educational personnel in order to face the day-in and day-out pressure of the classroom. Find a group of professionals who can talk about the stress of teaching and be able to discover positive strategies to deal with the students. Don't get caught up with a group of teachers that belittle students or simply complain about students. Find a support group that reviews new ideas and has had some success with their students.

8. **Eat breakfast and lunch.** Teachers are rushed in the morning, but breakfast is the most important meal for everyone. In most schools teachers usually have only a thirty-minute lunch period. This brief lunch time is often reduced further by picking up the students in the lunch room. Nevertheless, eat lunch. Teaching is a high-energy profession and good nutrition is important. It is amazing how much better you will feel when you have had a good lunch.

DISCIPLINE PLANS FOR MIDDLE SCHOOL TEAMS

The Great Thing about Teamwork is That You Always Have Someone on Your Side!

It has been well documented at the middle school level that a team approach to the environment benefits the preadolescent learner in the affective and cognitive domains. When teachers join as a team and share a common approach to discipline, everyone benefits! A team of teachers should be a seamless wall of behavioral expectations with allowances for individual differences. The differences between the teaching team members are best worked out between the teachers privately and amicably. This approach among team members demonstrates mutual respect and sensitivity. The following vignette is an example of how a team can agree about issues that affect the learning environment.

The Worst Time of Day ... Last Period. Can This Team Be Saved?

The team was very concerned about the increase of behavior problems that occurred in the last class period of the day. Office referrals had increased, and the teachers were exhausted. Mrs. Kirby and Mrs. McMillan came up with the idea that behavior might improve if the team switched the times when they had certain classes. They proposed that on Mondays, Wednesday, and Fridays, instead of always conducting the last class of the day (their sixth-period class) from 2:00–3:00, they would switch it with first period. This would mean that teachers would have their first-period class during the sixth-period time on those days. On Tuesdays and Thursdays they could also swap second and fifth periods. Third and fourth periods could not be swapped because of P.E. and lunch. These two teachers thought they had a great idea, so they met with the other two team members, Mr. Smith and Mr. Salato. Mr. Smith and Mr. Salato were not impressed. It seemed to be very confusing, and they stated that they did not want to do this. Mrs. Kirby and Mrs. McMillan were disappointed, but they did see the other teachers' point of view.

Later that day, Mr. Salato came down to Mrs. McMillan's room with a counterproposal. He, too, was discouraged with the students' conduct. He proposed that rather than switching the classes on Monday, Wednesdays, and Fridays, they could swap first and sixth period for an entire week. All homeroom teachers could discuss the change with their students on Monday morning. The new schedule could be posted on each teacher's door, and the students could be given an individual copy of the schedule.

This was a great idea! The team began the plan on the following Monday and behavior improved. Mr. Salato's plan had a better structure than the first plan did.

This is a great example of teaming. Everyone listened and everyone kept an open mind. No one got angry. Anger would have shut down communication and caused hard feelings. This teaming effort resulted in everyone being helped. Behavior improved, and the team realized the power of a unified front!

Night School

If teachers agree, a team may decide to offer an after-school detention. This is an old-fashioned, tried and true method for discouraging student misbehavior and for giving students an opportunity to work quietly and complete homework. This strategy can be known as "Night School." A notification form is on the following page. This formal letter informs the parents of the team policy. The memo forms on page 20 can be used as a reminder to the student or for subsequent detentions. Memo forms may be kept on the "Dreaded Clipboard." (See page 72.)

Pros of Night School

- It's an alternative to corporal punishment.
- It's an approach that causes students to complete assignments.
- The team of teachers could share night school responsibilities.
- Two or more teachers may choose to supervise Night School together. While there, they could enjoy a snack, do creative planning, or catch up on paperwork together.

Cons of Night School

- Arrangements would have to be made with a parent to insure that the students get home safely.
- Someone on the team would have to monitor the night school area.
- If the student did not report to night school a more severe punishment would have to be administered.

NIGHT SCHOOL NOTIFICATION FORM

Date _____

Dear Parent(s) or Guardian,

It is the policy of the _____ Team that students who report to school without homework, who waste class time, who disrupt the learning process, or who repeatedly break team rules will be asked to spend time in after-school detention. This practice is in an effort to avoid In-School Suspension or Out-of-School Suspension. Students who do not serve their time after school are in danger of receiving an office referral.

Detention will be service after school in _____ room. Students will work quietly from _____ P.M. to _____ P.M. Be certain to have a ride here no later than _____ P.M. Students are not supervised after this time.

Your child, _____ , has been assigned to after school detention for

_____

_____

_____

_____

_____

_____

_____ .

Please sign below giving your permission for your child to stay after school on _____ and confirming that you will have a ride here by _____ P.M.

Thank you for your support.

Sincerely,

_____

_____
Parent Signature   Date

Memo:

This is to verify that _____is invited/required

to stay after school on _____ from _____ until _____ .

Your child's difficulties include: _____

_____

_____

Signed _____

I will pick up my child after school at _____ P.M.

Signed _____

- -

Memo:

This is to verify that _____is invited/required

to stay after school on _____ from _____ until _____ .

Your child's difficulties include: _____

_____

_____

Signed _____

I will pick up my child after school at _____ P.M.

Signed _____

- -

Memo:

This is to verify that _____is invited/required

to stay after school on _____ from _____ until _____ .

Your child's difficulties include: _____

_____

_____

Signed _____

I will pick up my child after school at _____ P.M.

Signed _____

PARENT COMMUNICATION WITH THE TEAM

It is essential that a team of teachers remain in touch with the parents of students who are having academic or behavior problems at school. By using a daily progress report, parents and teachers may recognize patterns of success and failure that will assist the team in designing an intervention and help parents use encouragement and other rewards at home.

It is easy for students to become dependent on the daily sheets, however. All parties must understand that the sheet is a temporary intervention and an investigation tool. Parents and teachers must agree on a time limit for students to use the sheet, and then the weaning process must be carefully monitored for possible slips.

The **Progress at a Glance** on page 23 is a short form for one week of monitoring. This may provide a graceful, gentle method for an important move toward independence and self-monitoring for the student.

The **Weekly Progress Report** on page 24 is for a general overview of behavior. It could summarize a week or up to a six-week period.

The **Team Progress Report** on page 25 is a summary of conduct and grades. This is effective as a midterm report to the parents.

The following letter outlines everyone's responsibilities and gives suggestions for taking best advantage of the information gathered on the daily progress sheet.

DAILY PROGRESS REPORT LETTER

Date _____

To the Parents/Guardian of _____

We are happy to provide a daily progress report on your child's behavior, work habits, and attitudes. The sheet is very useful in monitoring completion of homework and class work and discovering patterns of success and failure. To maximize the benefits of having this information, it is vital that all parties be aware of their responsibilities and commitments. Parents are the child's most important support in the success of the experiment, so the suggestions below may prove helpful to you as you encourage your child's academic and social success. Remember to keep rewards and consequences small enough so that the child is starting with a clean slate every day. This will encourage the student to persevere. It takes time to break bad habits.

The goal of this sheet is to make your child an independent and self-disciplined learner. Three weeks of using the daily progress sheet is a good gauge for evaluating progress. If used longer than that, it may become a crutch and promote dependence on adults.

It is the responsibility of the student to:

- make every effort to comply with the agreed expectations of teachers and parents

- bring the sheet to each teacher politely and request that the teacher complete it

- take the sheet home and go over the day's evaluation with a parent or guardian

- return the signed sheet to the school the next day

It is the responsibility of the parent or guardian to:

- explain to the child the purpose of the sheet and the home routine for going over the sheet

- encourage the child to meet the expectations listed on the sheet

- sign the sheet each night (Your signature does not imply approval. It simply guarantees that you have seen the sheet.)

It is the responsibility of the teacher to:

- explain the school routine for making sure the sheet is completed

- fill out the sheet near the end of the class period

- encourage the student to meet the expectations listed on the sheet

- provide positive and negative comments to give the parents an accurate picture of the day

Sincerely,

_____

Positive Classroom Management
©1997 by Incentive Publications, Inc., Nashville, TN

PROGRESS AT A GLANCE

Name _____ Date _____

Subject	In Class on Time (Yes or No)	Conduct (S+, S, S-, U)	Homework Complete (Yes or No)	Comments
Math	_____	_____	_____	_____
Lang. Arts	_____	_____	_____	_____
Science	_____	_____	_____	_____
Soc. Stu.	_____	_____	_____	_____

Parent's Signature _____

Name _____ Date _____

Subject	In Class on Time (Yes or No)	Conduct (S+, S, S-, U)	Homework Complete (Yes or No)	Comments
Math	_____	_____	_____	_____
Lang. Arts	_____	_____	_____	_____
Science	_____	_____	_____	_____
Soc. Stu.	_____	_____	_____	_____

Parent's Signature _____

Name _____ Date _____

Subject	In Class on Time (Yes or No)	Conduct (S+, S, S-, U)	Homework Complete (Yes or No)	Comments
Math	_____	_____	_____	_____
Lang. Arts	_____	_____	_____	_____
Science	_____	_____	_____	_____
Soc. Stu.	_____	_____	_____	_____

Parent's Signature _____

Name _____ Date _____

Subject	In Class on Time (Yes or No)	Conduct (S+, S, S-, U)	Homework Complete (Yes or No)	Comments
Math	_____	_____	_____	_____
Lang. Arts	_____	_____	_____	_____
Science	_____	_____	_____	_____
Soc. Stu.	_____	_____	_____	_____

Parent's Signature _____

Name _____ Date _____

Subject	In Class on Time (Yes or No)	Conduct (S+, S, S-, U)	Homework Complete (Yes or No)	Comments
Math	_____	_____	_____	_____
Lang. Arts	_____	_____	_____	_____
Science	_____	_____	_____	_____
Soc. Stu.	_____	_____	_____	_____

Parent's Signature _____

WEEKLY PROGRESS REPORT

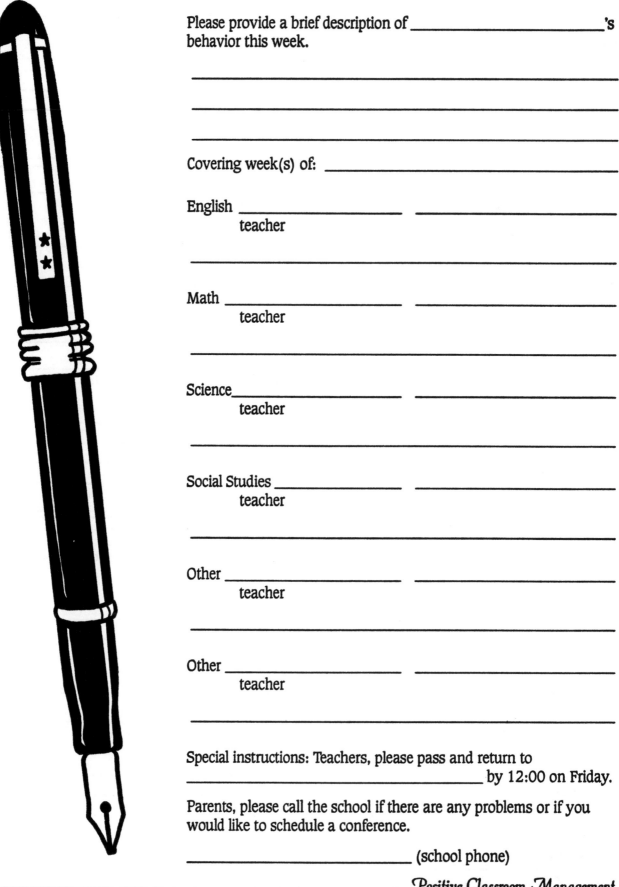

Please provide a brief description of _____'s behavior this week.

_____

_____

_____

Covering week(s) of: _____

English _____   _____
       teacher

_____

Math _____   _____
      teacher

_____

Science_____   _____
      teacher

_____

Social Studies _____   _____
      teacher

_____

Other _____   _____
      teacher

_____

Other _____   _____
      teacher

_____

Special instructions: Teachers, please pass and return to
_____ by 12:00 on Friday.

Parents, please call the school if there are any problems or if you would like to schedule a conference.

_____ (school phone)

_____ *Positive Classroom Management*

TEAM PROGRESS REPORT

Student Name _____ Date _____

Grade average at this time in the grading period:

Math _____

Language _____

Social Studies _____

Science _____

If a comment is ✔ (checked), this is a characteristic of your child.

Comments:	Math	Lang.	S. Studies	Science
Excellent Behavior				
Positive Attitude				
Enjoys Helping				
Works Well with Others				
Shows Leadership				
Low Daily Grades				
Low Test Grades				
Needs Supplies				
Does not Complete Homework				
Needs to Improve Conduct				
Needs to Improve Attendance				
Other				

Please sign this form and return it to your child's homeroom teacher.

Signature _____ Date _____

The team of teachers is available _____ .

For a conference, call _____

Positive Classroom Management _____ 25

©1997 by Incentive Publications, Inc., Nashville, TN

CHART WORK

Someone once said, "If the teacher doesn't have an agenda for the class period, there are thirty kids who do!" Planning how class time is spent is very critical to managing students' behavior.

One simple strategy is Chart Work. Each day write five questions on one page of a chart table. The questions should require short answers. They should be questions that the students can answer without your assistance. Design the questions to take no more than five minutes of class time.

In order for Chart Work to be effective in the management of student behavior, follow these important points:

- On bright paper run a Chart Work sheet (see page 28) for each student. Distribute the sheets to each student, and instruct the students to place the sheets in the very front of their notebooks or folders.

- Inform the students that each day when they enter the classroom they are to begin working on their Chart Work. You can reinforce the importance of beginning promptly by:

  - verbally praising the students who begin immediately

  - permitting the students who started right away to have one free answer (This could mean that the students would have to complete only four out of five questions, or the students can answer one of the five questions incorrectly and still receive full credit.)

- In the beginning set a timer to let the students know when they must be done with the Chart Work. This strategy will let the students know that they cannot waste class time. When the timer goes off, finished or not, inform the students that Chart Work time has ended.

- It is important to grade the Chart Work daily. It is best to let the students grade their own papers. Quickly call on students to answer the Chart Work questions. (This also allows you to conduct a quick review and assess the students' retention of the material.) Ask students to score their work by marking down the number they answered correctly out of the five questions. If you suspect that the students are cheating when grading their work, follow one of these strategies:

  - Distribute red pens to each student. During the grading of Chart Work each student must be using a red pen.

  - Make the students swap papers and grade each other's work.

- If a student does not have his or her Chart Work paper, they can be given another one, but they lose the points from the previous work they have completed. Don't get trapped by wasting class time dealing with this problem.

- At the end of the week instruct the students to total how many are correct out of the 25 possible. Multiply the total by 4, and count this score as a daily grade.

- As an extension of this activity, allow students who finish class work early to write five questions for Chart Work the next day. This activity permits them to think of good questions about the material learned in class, and it frees you from constantly having to provide questions.

The Chart Work Strategy works well if it is used consistently in the classroom. The students learn that class begins in a specific way each day. This strategy insures that eventually all students will get out a pencil and begin working without your daily prompting.

Occasionally, as you start the lesson, if everyone has worked hard on the chart work, surprise the students by saying, "This is surely the best class in the United States. Everyone was doing EXACTLY what I have asked. Everyone gets a perfect score on Chart Work today." This example of positive reinforcement works every time!

"... EVERYONE WAS DOING <u>EXACTLY</u> WHAT I HAVE ASKED !..."

IT'S CHART WORK TIME

Date _____

  1. _____

  2. _____

  3. _____

  4. _____

  5. _____

Daily Total _____

Date _____

  1. _____

  2. _____

  3. _____

  4. _____

  5. _____

Daily Total _____

Date _____

  1. _____

  2. _____

  3. _____

  4. _____

  5. _____

Daily Total _____

Date _____

  1. _____

  2. _____

  3. _____

  4. _____

  5. _____

Daily Total _____

Date _____

  1. _____

  2. _____

  3. _____

  4. _____

  5. _____

Daily Total _____

Weekly Total _____

Name _____

_____ *Positive Classroom Management*

CELEBRATION WEEK

Certain weeks of the year lend themselves to excitement and, unfortunately, to rowdiness. To keep the week calm, announce the observance of Celebration Week. Celebration Week may be celebrated as often as needed and in an infinite number of ways. A sample of celebrations is listed below. It is useful to start out the week with a celebration that is simple to achieve and then to progress to a level that requires more and more self-control. The week ends with a celebration of simple refreshments, a short video, or outdoor games.

Provide a sheet to stamp, punch, or initial. Each student keeps his or her own sheet, which avoids transference of rewards among students. Decide on an acceptable level of success, how absences will be handled, and what students will do if they do not qualify for the reward. Post the rewards a day or two in advance of the designated week to assure a high level of success. Announce the reward, and let the festivities begin.

Monday—Locker Check Day. Students who celebrate by cleaning their lockers will have their sheets stamped.

Tuesday—Punctuality Day. Students who celebrate by arriving on time to all classes and return promptly from restroom breaks will have their sheets stamped.

Wednesday—Preparedness Day. Students who celebrate by having all books, materials, and assignments will have their sheets stamped.

Thursday—Quietude Day. Students who celebrate by maintaining quiet in the classroom, hall, restroom, and cafeteria will have their sheets stamped.

Friday—Etiquette Day. Students who celebrate by using their best manners will have their sheets stamped.

Celebrant _____ A stamp or check in each box indicates success!

M	T	W	Th	F

ANNOUNCING CELEBRATION WEEK

Dates _____ to _____

MONDAY—Locker Check Day

Students who celebrate by cleaning their lockers will have their sheets stamped.

TUESDAY—Punctuality Day

Students who celebrate by arriving on time to all classes and returning promptly from restroom breaks will have their sheets stamped.

WEDNESDAY—Preparedness Day

Students who celebrate by having all books, materials, and assignments will have their sheets stamped.

THURSDAY—Quietude Day

Students who celebrate by maintaining quiet in the classroom, hall, restroom, and cafeteria will have their sheets stamped.

FRIDAY—Etiquette Day

Students who celebrate by using their best manners will have their sheets stamped.

Positive Classroom Management

THE FIFTEEN-MINUTE COUNTDOWN GAME

At times an entire group of students is very disruptive. The students are out of their seats, talking without permission, and engaging in disruptive behaviors. An effective strategy is The Fifteen-Minute Countdown Game.

To play the game:

- Without the students' knowledge, divide the class into two teams. The easiest way to do this is to reassign the students' seats into rows. If there are four rows in the class, make one team the first two rows and the last two rows the other team. Be certain to divide the worst-behaving students evenly between the two teams.

- Determine what behaviors are causing the greatest problems in the classroom. Attempt to keep the list to no more than three problem areas. Let's say talking, out-of-seat behavior, and inappropriate touching are real problem areas. Define the behaviors clearly. The defining of the behaviors will help you and the students grasp what is appropriate and what is not appropriate. It also eliminates "gray" areas. For example:

Talking: Talking or whispering without permission. This also includes: talking when one's hand is raised (before one is called on), calling out to you or other students, blurting out answers, and making animal sounds.

Out-of-seat behavior: Leaving one's seat without permission. This includes: throwing away trash and sharpening pencils without prior permission.

Inappropriate Touching: Touching another student in a way that disrupts the student. This includes: hitting, kicking, moving one's desk to touch another student's, or turning around in one's desk to bother other students.

- Using the chart on page 33, record the behavior of each team for a fifteen-minute period. The first three times the behavior is recorded, do not let the students know what is being tallied. This data will provide a baseline for the game. The baseline will help determine if the game is effective in curbing behavioral problems.

The chart used for recording has a column for each team. Each time a team member performs one of the undesirable behaviors, a tally mark is placed in that team's column.

- Once a baseline is determined, a goal is set for the class. For example, if, during the baseline phase, each team averaged ten undesirable behaviors in fifteen minutes, you might set a goal that only five infractions should occur once the students are made aware of the game.

- Once an appropriate goal is set, explain the game to the students in the following manner:

  1. The class has been divided into two teams in order for the class to play The Fifteen-Minute Countdown Game. For example, rows 1 and 2 are the Blue Team and rows 3 and 4 are the Red Team.

  2. This game will be played only during a specific fifteen-minute period each day.

  3. It is possible for both teams to win the game.

  4. To win the game, each team should commit no more than five offenses during the fifteen-minute period. (At this point, clearly explain the three infractions. You should make certain the students thoroughly understand what behaviors will result in a rule being broken. The students should understand what permission means.)

  5. Whenever one of the team members breaks one of the rules, a mark will be placed on the recording sheet against that team.

  6. A team or both teams can win if they receive five or fewer marks against them.

  7. If a team or teams win(s) they will receive, for example, three minutes of free time at the end of the period.

- It is best to record the marks on the board. Tell the students that you are the only one who will determine if rules have been broken. Arguing with you will automatically result in a mark against the team.

- Inform the class as to when The Fifteen-Minute Countdown Game will be played. Conduct a normal lesson during the time period. The only difference is that you will mark on the board when a rule has been broken. DO NOT STOP CLASS and discuss the mark. Place it on the board and keep going. Refuse to discuss the marks at that time. Group processing of the results should occur after the fifteen-minute time period.

- When the game is over, announce the winner(s). Inform the winner(s) of their reward(s).

- Repeat the game each day for a period of seven days. At this time, if behavior has improved, you may want to discontinue the game. If behavior has not improved, discuss with the students how the class could change the game in order to help them improve their classroom behavior. Students might want a new reward, or they might want to change the make-up of the teams. Student input could be a valuable insight into the behavioral problems in the classroom.

THE FIFTEEN-MINUTE COUNTDOWN GAME

The three undesirable behaviors are:

Undesirable Behavior #1 is _____

It is defined as: _____

_____

_____

_____

Undesirable Behavior #2 is _____

It is defined as: _____

_____

_____

_____

Undesirable Behavior #3 is _____

It is defined as: _____

_____

_____

_____

Beginning Game Time: _____

Ending Game Time: _____

Team 1	Team 2

Strategies and Activities for Positive Student Behavior

TEACHING STUDENTS TO BE SELF-SUFFICIENT

Students bring their worries to school. In addition, they are aware of problems that other students are bearing. By learning to use the yellow pages, students may gain independence, develop a sense of empowerment, and find important resources for healthy living. Hopefully, they will transfer this confidence to the study of their textbooks. Try the following questions as a scavenger hunt through the yellow pages. Some communities even publish Youth Yellow Pages, and these are rich sources of information for teenagers.

To create a curiosity about community resources, assign the Yellow Pages Scavenger Hunt as homework or collect yellow pages just before recycling time and try this activity in class.

Should we look under ... "C" for car, "L" for limousine, or "Y" for "Yikes!"?

YELLOW PAGES SCAVENGER HUNT

Look through the yellow pages and complete the following activities:

1. List two things that might be fun for teenagers to do and the phone numbers they might call for information about these activities.

   _____

   _____

2. Use the Table of Contents to find the page containing information about family problems. List two agencies and their phone numbers below.

   _____

   _____

3. Find a number for a crisis intervention center. Write it below.

   _____

4. What number would you tell a friend to call who had questions about homelessness?

   _____

5. What number would you call if you had questions about juvenile law?

   _____

6. Where would you call if your friend had questions about school attendance?

   _____

7. Running away from home is a very dangerous and frightening experience. What number should your friend call if he or she is thinking about running away?

   _____

8. Is there a number for a homework hot line in your community? If so, write it below.

   _____

9. Find a phone number for a club related to one of your interests. Write it below. Check here _____ if you belong to that club.

   _____

10. Look in the Table of Contents for "safe houses." Define what a "safe house" is and write a phone number for one in your community.

    _____

Name _____ **Date** _____

NAME TAGS

Name tags are an inexpensive and powerful symbol of responsibility and self-esteem. Name tags may designate a privilege or an official capacity. They can give the wearer authority and a hall pass at the same time. Below are a number of designs for name tags that scratch the surface of possibilities.

LUNCH HOST/HOSTESS

or

TEAM EMISSARY
MAY I RUN AN ERRAND FOR YOU?

or

INSTRUCTIONAL ASSISTANT

or

CLERICAL ASSISTANT

HONOR STUDENT

Make up your own designs for Diplomat, Engineer, & Accountant!

JOURNALIST OR SECRETARY

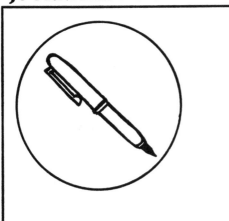

HEALTH INSPECTOR

LUNCH GUEST

ENVIRONMENTALIST
I BELIEVE IN CLEAN LIVING.

or

HORTICULTURIST

LIBRARIAN

A LETTER OF RECOMMENDATION

When you notice special talent in a student, a letter of recommendation is in order. Your letter can act as a liaison for students who are interested in volunteering, but are nervous about approaching the appropriate staff member to make the arrangements to do so. It can be particularly helpful for students who are shy or socially awkward.

Below is a sample letter written for a student who was transferring to another school under stressful circumstances. Due to family tragedy, this student had a history of numerous transitions, and his records were sometimes trailing. You may wish to write letters of recommendation for many reasons and hope that the written word may reap many good rewards for students for years to come. Copies of the letter are often appreciated by parents.

Centerville Middle School
1500 Hill Rd.
Centerville, North Dakota 99999
June 1, 1997

To whom it may concern:

I am delighted to recommend Andy to you as a capable, creative, and conscientious student. Andy has a lively curiosity, a gentle spirit, and a strong work ethic. He is an asset to any class, and he knows how to seize educational opportunity with enthusiasm. His grades and standardized test scores support this highly subjective opinion.

If I may provide further information to you, please call me at home or at Two Rivers Middle School.

Sincerely,

Barbara A. Jones

Barbara Ann Jones

POSITIVE SCHOOL SURVIVAL SKILLS
WITH POSTERS

Using posters is an effective method to prompt positive behavior. The posters on this page and the following page can be used to remind the student of strategies that make others feel positive about the request. The poster on page 42 is helpful when a student is demonstrating poor behaviors. Prompting the student to read the poster may encourage "rethinking" of his or her behaviors. The Chinese Proverb on page 43 is helpful when discussing proper actions.

These things will help you get what you want:

Smiling
Polite Requests
Written Requests
Smiling
Offering Alternatives
Explaining
Following Instructions
Smiling
Thinking
Waiting Calmly
Smiling

©1997 by Incentive Publications, Inc., Nashville, TN

These things will not help you get what you want:

Pouting

Yelling

Demanding

Pouting

Disobeying Rules

Sleeping in Class

Omitting Homework

Pouting

Forgetting Materials

Blaming Others

Calling Out

Pouting

If
ten thousand
people do
a foolish
thing,
it is still
a foolish
thing.

–Chinese Proverb

LUNCH IN THE ROOM

Wise teachers know that some discipline problems arise because students are trying to gain the attention of other students. A student who is having difficulty making friends may need an excuse to reach out to other students in an appropriate manner. One method for encouraging students to include shy students is to permit students to eat lunch in your classroom.

Discreetly give a student who is having trouble making friends a coupon for eating lunch in the room and say that the student may invite two students to join him or her for a quick lunch. Students may be permitted to listen to the radio or even to watch television. This coupon gives students a little leverage with their peers.

An "Eating Lunch in the Room" coupon may also be used as a reward or a special prize in a drawing. Also see name tag ideas on page 39.

LUNCH IN THE ROOM

You are entitled to eat

your lunch in the classroom.

Enjoy the educational ambience

of room _____.

You may invite two of your friends

to share this dining experience with you.

_____

Teacher's Signature

FIELD TRIPS

Educational trips are a vital part of the academic program of any middle school, but teachers know that excitement sometimes translates into uncontrolled, dangerous behavior on a field trip.

Unfortunately, sometimes there is a temptation to leave some students at school when taking a field trip. There may be a justification for omitting students from a roller skating or bowling trip if the trip is a reward for good behavior and if it has limited educational value. However, it might prove valuable to analyze whether or not the same students are losing the reward every time. If so, these trips may not motivate those students.

When trips are an integral part of the unit of study or their cultural value is part of an educational experience, you will want to explore every opportunity for taking all students regardless of their usual patterns of negative behavior. Consider Ms. Arnold's dilemma. She was planning a unit on Civil War history. She arranged for a tour of an antebellum home that had been used as a hospital during an important battle. In spite of her excitement she had four students whose patterns of impulsive behavior gave her pause. Ms. Arnold also realized that all four of these students were largely unmotivated except for lessons involving hands-on learning. The field trip would be the most meaningful part of the unit for each of these students. Ms. Arnold decided to evaluate these students' behavior to look for patterns. If particular types of events were prompting bad behaviors, she could find ways to help the students. Ms. Arnold kept referrals and anecdotal remarks on note cards. She reviewed the following cards. (See documentation ideas on page 14 and "Anecdotal Cards" on page 59.)

Pommel, Tamika

9/10 —negative comments, warned, cont. time out 15 min.,
      loud, negative comments, finally stopped.

9/11 —absent, called, mother unaware of absence

9/12 —returned to school, ISS due to bus problem

9/13 —suspended

9/14 —Progress! Loved the card game! Perfect behavior,
      sent a positive note home to mother !

Ms. Arnold had to smile because in spite of Tamika's volatile nature, she was likable and she couldn't resist manipulatives, games, or flashy visuals. More than once, Ms. Arnold had been concerned that Tamika was close to fighting. She deliberately provoked other students in the hall and the bathroom. On the other hand, her learning style would favor her on the field trip.

Leonard's card held a different challenge.

Grady, Leonard

9/12 —unprepared, warned, loaned paper and pencil, sent note home to mother

9/13 —note returned, mother asked for a few days to gather materials

9/28 —unprepared, note home

10/1 —late, unprepared, no HW

Leonard's problems, while frustrating and persistent, held little peril for a field trip disaster.

Timothy's card was revealing to Ms. Arnold. She had already noted that Timothy was absent almost every Monday.

Lomas, Timothy

9/13 —sleeping, very angry when disturbed. Refused to accept paper or pencil from Janet

9/20 —unprepared, very slow to start assgt. after obtaining materials

9/28 —threatening Tamika (Yikes)

9/29 —unprepared, sleeping, found biography of Lincoln in his desk, defensive when I asked him about book, said it was his from library

9/30 —very interested in Gettysburg Address bulletin bd, asked to help

---

Timothy might be intrigued by the subject matter. This was a hopeful sign. Ms. Arnold grinned as she recalled putting up the bulletin board with Timothy's help. He knew so much about Lincoln, and he told her that he had Civil War toy soldiers at home. He and his uncle reenacted battles on the den floor. If ever Timothy might hold it together, it would be on this trip. Ms. Arnold asked Timothy if his uncle might chaperone on the trip. Timothy tried to hide his enthusiasm, but he "guessed he would ask."

Natalie also had problems that erupted almost daily. Natalie was a student who held extra challenges for Ms. Arnold.

Wilson, Natalie

9/10 —tardy, lingering in rest room, primping

9/11 —tardy, knocked student's papers as she passed, office referral

9/20 —loud negative comments in hall re: Angela's new hairstyle, conf. in hall

9/28 —loud negative comments in cafeteria re: Ms. Kelly's sweater,
         called mother

9/29 —loud, negative comments in restroom re: Janet's teeth, office referral

---

Natalie had a learning disability, and she hid it carefully by covering her difficulties with hostility. She made every effort to linger in the hall, at her locker, in the cafeteria, or in the rest room. School policy dictated that the third tardy required an office referral, and after several days of In-School Suspension (I.S.S.), the tardies had decreased, but had not stopped. Natalie was obsessed with her looks, pulling out make-up and combing her hair at every opportunity. Her primping habit was not appreciated in I.S.S., and she received extra days for a long, loud argument with the teacher. Her impulsive behavior and unkind remarks to students and adults showed that Natalie might do something dangerous or embarrassing on the trip.

Ms. Arnold realized that her students' problems were diverse and that various solutions would be needed. She decided to ask Timothy's uncle to chaperone, trusting that their mutual interest and Timothy's respect for his uncle would be a restraining force for him. Leonard's tendency to be unprepared and unconcerned held little problem in the field trip setting. Tamika and Natalie still presented a challenge to Ms. Arnold. She called Tamika's parents to see if either could chaperone, but Mrs. Pommel was ill and Mr. Pommel lived in another state. She decided to make an appointment with her principal, Dr. Ray, and discuss available options.

Dr. Ray agreed that the girls were a handful, but said that she would not be able to accompany the group due to a scheduled meeting. She offered to arrange for an assistant to Natalie's special education teacher to accompany her on the trip and suggested that Natalie and the assistant ride in a car that would be able to leave early if Natalie grew restless. As for Tamika, Ms. Arnold knew that if she missed the trip she might not garner much from the entire unit. In addition, Dr. Ray and Ms. Arnold realized that the class would need a number of parent and volunteer chaperones, and Dr. Ray agreed to search for other volunteers while Ms. Arnold began phoning parents.

Ms. Arnold felt that her four special challenges would need to be close to her during the field trip. By making careful arrangements and preparing well, Ms. Arnold felt confident that she could include all of her students on the excursion. Dr. Ray and Ms. Arnold reviewed the basics of field trip success. Ms. Arnold worked carefully to prepare her students as the day of the trip approached.

FIELD TRIP FORMS

Questionnaire

You may choose to use the questionnaire on page 49 to encourage students to remain focused during an educational field trip. Questions with specific relevance to the trip may be added by the teacher.

Field Trip Contracts and Letter to Parents of Children with Chronic Behavior Problems

For students who have chronic behavior problems, the letter on page 50 is useful if it is sent home to parents several days before the trip. Most teachers will not send this letter to the entire class. Attach the Field Trip Contract (page 51) to the letter home. This will make the parents aware of the behavior expectations.

Field Trip Quiz

You may choose to give the Field Trip Quiz (page 52) to students whose behavior has been questionable. Discuss each item, and patiently lead students into an awareness of the need to positively represent themselves, their families, and their school.

Field Trip Evaluation

Students may be encouraged to remain in good self-control during a field trip when they know that they will be using a form for self-evaluation, peer evaluation, and chaperone evaluation. The form on page 53 is a simple way to do this type of evaluation. The self-evaluation helps to remind students of their responsibilities on a research trip. Be sure that chaperones have a sample form and that they know they will be asked to evaluate student behavior. Students are to fill out their portions, ask a friend to fill out the peer evaluation portion, and then politely ask the chaperone to fill out the last portion and return it to the teacher. Make sure students are wearing name tags so that chaperones and guides may identify them correctly.

FIELD TRIP QUESTIONNAIRE

Researcher _____ .

The purpose of our trip is _____

_____

_____ .

Our destination is _____ .

We are traveling by _____ , and the operator is _____ .

Bus # _____ or van color _____

My chaperone is _____ .

My journal entry topic for today is " _____

_____ ."

My To Do List

☐ Write a thank-you note to our guide.

☐ Write a thank-you note to my chaperone.

☐ Make a word bank of vocabulary discovered on the trip.
   (Spelling can be corrected later at school.)

☐ Make a puzzle of words or images I discovered on the trip.

☐ Make a rough sketch of the building(s) we visited.

FIELD TRIP LETTER

Date _____

Dear Parent(s)/Guardians,

Our team is preparing for a unit of study which includes a field trip. We hope to include all of our students and to extend this opportunity to everyone. There are concerns, however, for the safety, comfort, and educational benefit of all participants. Students must be counted on to exhibit their very best behavior and to demonstrate their good judgment for an extended period of time prior to the trip. All students who have demonstrated consistent, reliable behavior and positive attitudes are eligible. Students who have had difficulty in the past with following directions, sustaining productive work habits, demonstrating positive behavior, or using acceptable manners or language, are required to show their willingness to grow and learn by maintaining the attached Field Trip Contract.

In order to be eligible for the field trip experience, students must reach at least an 85% success rate in each category for five days. Students who succeed in this effort (and we hope that will be everyone) are welcome to attend and to participate fully in the events. Students who do not meet the requirements will be provided with an alternate assignment at school. This activity will involve research at school to complement our research in the field. Students will read, outline information, compile charts and graphs, report on their findings, and design a presentation of their results.

Please encourage your child to demonstrate the behaviors shown on the Field Trip Contract.

Sincerely,

_____

Positive Classroom Management
©1997 by Incentive Publications, Inc., Nashville, TN

FIELD TRIP CONTRACT

For the next five days you will be rated on specific positive behaviors. If you can earn 85 points out of a possible 100, you can go on the field trip. Each day you can earn up to 20 points. Each desirable behavior is worth up to 4 points. Earn 4 points in each category for all five days and you will receive a 100 on this contract.

Remember—85 points and you are on your way!!!!!!

Name _____

	Day 1	Day 2	Day 3	Day 4	Day 5
Remains in area					
Arrives in class on time and is prepared					
Assignments completed					
Positive language/ behavior					
Follows directions and remains on task					
Daily Total					

Grand Total [ ]

Key

4 points = Excellent behavior
3 points = Good behavior
2 points = Okay behavior
1 point = Some problems, but improved during the day
0 points = Unacceptable behavior

FIELD TRIP QUIZ

Name _____ Date _____

Answer each question with a T for True or an F for False.

___ 1. I enjoy the opportunity to travel on a field trip.

___ 2. I understand that I am representing myself, my family, my school, and my team.

___ 3. It is impossible for me to keep my voice low.

___ 4. It is possible for me to keep my hands to myself.

___ 5. I am self-controlled.

___ 6. I control my own attitude.

___ 7. The bus driver is not a person in authority.

___ 8. My family thinks it is important for me to behave positively on a field trip.

___ 9. Adults have to make me behave; I cannot do it myself.

___ 10. I should have a good time on the field trip.

___ 11. Everyone should have a good time on the field trip.

___ 12. It is my responsibility to help on the trip.

___ 13. Cleaning up is my responsibility.

___ 14. My teachers even take students who misbehave on field trips.

___ 15. I hope I will be able to hear all the stories, jokes, and directions given on the trip.

___ 16. I hope everyone will behave pleasantly and enjoy the trip.

Think about the following, and then write your answer.

Name three things you can do to help make the field trip pleasant for everyone.

1. _____

2. _____

3. _____

Name two things you can do to help clean up.

1. _____

2. _____

Name one thing you can do to help someone with special needs.

1. _____

_____ *Positive Classroom Management*

SELF-EVALUATION

Name _____

Date _____ Destination _____

5 = Consistently positive   4 = Almost always positive   3 = Usually good
2 = Needs improvement   1 = Consistently negative

Rate yourself on your behavior today. 0–5

_____ Manners

_____ Listening and paying attention

_____ Following directions

_____ No gum, headphones, toys

_____ Prepared

Ask a friend to rate you. 0–5

_____ Manners

_____ Listening and paying attention

_____ Following directions

_____ No gum, headphones, toys

_____ Prepared

Ask your chaperone to rate you and turn in form to teacher. 0–5

_____ Manners

_____ Listening and paying attention

_____ Following directions

_____ No gum, headphones, toys

_____ Prepared

A teacher will rate you and return this form to you. 0–5

_____ Manners

_____ Listening and paying attention

_____ Following directions

_____ No gum, headphones, toys

_____ Prepared

100 points are possible. Your score _____

Parent Signature_____

FIELD TRIP CHECKLIST

In order to insure that a field trip will be safe, organized, and fun, good planning is essential. Use the Field Trip Checklist as a guide in your planning.

- ☐ Preview the site and keep an eye out for distractions and hazards.
- ☐ Maintain a low ratio of students to chaperones.
- ☐ Make arrangements for students with special needs.
- ☐ Make arrangements for lunch and snacks.
- ☐ Make a plan in case of inclement weather.
- ☐ Calculate the cost of the trip per student.
- ☐ Write the permission note and have another teacher proofread it, looking for glitches.
- ☐ Collect money, carefully keeping track of students' permission slips.
- ☐ Arrange for scholarships for students who cannot afford the cost.
- ☐ Outline the rules for field trip behavior the day before the trip.
- ☐ Describe your expectations of students when delays occur.
- ☐ Give students a list of items they need and another list of items they must not bring.
- ☐ Make sure all buses, cars, and vans have clear, written directions to the destination.
- ☐ Assign groups to vehicles.
- ☐ Make a plan in case a chaperone or a driver doesn't show up.
- ☐ Make name tags for all students and chaperones.
- ☐ Explain expectations for bus, car, and sidewalk behavior.
- ☐ Design groups so that students who provoke each other are separated.
- ☐ Color code groups so chaperones can keep track of their groups.
- ☐ Give each chaperone a list of names.
- ☐ Give each chaperone written directions.
- ☐ Assure chaperones that you expect students to follow their directions.
- ☐ Avoid a schedule that causes students to be hungry.
- ☐ Plan frequent restroom breaks.
- ☐ Make a handout to encourage students to focus on the highlights.
- ☐ Give the office an itinerary of your trip.

☐ Collect as many cellular phones as possible and exchange numbers.

☐ Designate a vehicle to be used in case of an emergency.

☐ Collect names and addresses to write thank-you notes to chaperones, scholarship donors, and guides.

Other "Things to Do" for the field trip: _____

_____

_____

_____

_____

_____

_____

_____

_____

_____

_____

_____

_____

_____

Phone numbers that are needed for field trip arrangements: _____

_____

_____

_____

_____

FIELD TRIP HOST AND HOSTESS

Students who have a history of minor behavior problems may be encouraged to remain with their chaperones by having responsibility for helping the chaperone. Students may be assigned to greet the chaperone, give materials to the chaperone, introduce other chaperones, and help the chaperone count students in the group. The following letter explains the duties of a host or hostess. (See Name Tags on page 38.)

FIELD TRIP HOST/HOSTESS

Dear _____

Please serve as host/hostess of your group. I have checked the duties I would like you to

perform. Your chaperones are: _____

_____

_____

☐ Greet your chaperone.

☐ Please welcome them and tell them how glad we are they could come.

☐ Give the attached materials to your chaperones.

☐ Pass out the name tags and make sure every student wears the name tag over his or her heart. The name tag is to be visible at all times.

☐ Introduce each student in your group by name to your chaperones.

☐ Distribute the field trip rules and self-evaluations.

☐ Throughout the day, assist your chaperones with names and faces.

☐ Be proud of yourself. We are proud of you.

TWENTY-FIVE ALTERNATIVES TO CORPORAL PUNISHMENT

1. **The Sunrise Club** is an effective tool to use if the school has a large number of students that either arrive early to school or can be brought early to school. The Sunrise Club is an early detention time ten minutes before school begins. To serve off the detention, students must arrive and be seated in the classroom before the school day starts. During this ten-minute detention, they are assigned to write about the infraction that resulted in their being assigned to the Sunrise Club. The students must describe alternative ways of handling the negative situation in the future. The detention area is only for "CLUB MEMBERS." No other students can be in the room during the "CLUB MEETING." (This CLUB business is a little bit "tongue in cheek," but it's fun to use the word club. You can refer to the club throughout the day with such statements as, "Hmmm, you must want to join the Sunrise Club" or "I have a special club into which I'm considering inducting you!")

2. **Trade-a-Student Plan** is a strategy that permits you to deal with disobedient students during the school day. You and another teacher agree that if a student disobeys in one of your rooms, you each have the option of moving that student to the other teacher's classroom. It is best if you both prepare a special desk for any incoming students. In order for the Trade-a-Student Plan to be effective, inform the students that if they are disobedient they will be moved to Teacher B's room. Teacher B has a desk in the first row reserved for a disobedient student. If a disobedient student is placed in Teacher B's room and the student is disruptive in that classroom, the student will immediately be given a harsher punishment (e.g., a call to parents, a visit to the principal). After the disobedient student has been in the other classroom for fifteen minutes, Teacher B will send him or her back to the original classroom. Why this strategy works is a mystery, but it does! Middle school students have a strong desire to be with their own peers, and this may be why displacing them is so effective. This strategy is especially effective if the classes vary in grade level. If the students in Teacher B's room are older, the disobedient student is often intimidated. If the students are younger, the disobedient student is uncomfortable being with "little kids." Removing the student also gives the teacher time to regroup before the student returns.

3. The old **"Sit in the Hall" Strategy** is still very effective. It seems to work best if a desk is placed in the hall and the student is given a task to complete. Inform the student that his or her behavior is unacceptable in the classroom, so he or she will need to go out in the hall and complete a brief assignment. When the student finishes the assignment, and if the student believes that he or she can follow the classroom rules, the student may come back in the room. You may want to maintain a standard assignment to give to such a student. The assignment should take the student about ten minutes. A typical assignment might be to require the student to copy the classroom rules. If the same student is placed in the hall often, this strategy is not effective for that student. Avoid removing students day after day.

4. **Calling a parent** is one method that helps insure a school/home connection. If this is a method that will be used, be certain that there are other methods in place that are encouraging parent involvement. You do not want a parent to receive only negative communication from the school. It is often helpful to call the parent and explain the problem and then place the student on the phone. A wise teacher will also call parents and brag about a student's accomplishments before placing the student on the phone.

5. **"I've got a secret"** is a great way to deal with a disruptive student. When a student is breaking a classroom rule, call the student up to the desk and say, "I've got a secret to tell you!" Whisper in the student's ear, for example, "If you do not stop doing _____ immediately, I'm going to have to punish you. You go back to your seat and begin following the classroom rules. If you do not comply, I will _____." This seems to work well, especially if the student realizes a severe punishment will occur if the behavior continues. Another advantage is that it gives the student a little attention when he or she is asked to come up to the teacher (which is sometimes all the student is interested in in the first place!) yet the conversation with the student is private. When this is a method of discipline that is used regularly, a student will often say, "I don't want to know the secret, I'll behave."

6. **Response cost** is a strategy that research has shown to be effective when dealing with impulsive students. The premise of this strategy is that the wrong response to a situation "costs" the student something of value. For example, if homework is not completed, it might cost the student five minutes of physical education class or some other desirable activity.

7. **Time-out Corner** is a tried and true method if administered correctly. The ideal situation is to place a desk in an isolated area of the classroom. This works best if the student is unable to see the other students. Be certain that the student can get out of the area on his or her own. In the typical classroom, a teacher generally places a desk behind a bookshelf or a filing cabinet. Don't leave the student isolated for long periods of time. Perhaps the old formula of one minute of isolation for each year of age is a good rule of thumb.

8. **Behavior Improvement Plan** is a strategy that is beneficial for the student that seems to have just recently started having behavior problems. Take the student to either the principal's office or the In-School Suspension room and explain to him or her that he or she must stay there for thirty minutes. During this time period, the student may choose to write an apology to the offended party (or parties) and must formulate a plan to improve his or her behavior. The student must return to the classroom with the assignment. If it is accepted by the teacher or principal, he or she may return to class. This plan is kept by you. If the same behavior occurs again, the assignment is given to the student and sent with him or her to the office. This shows that the student is unable to self-correct the behavior and a more severe intervention is needed. See page 64 for a sample form.

9. **Become a broken record.** When students are "stuck" on a minor point of order and they want to split hairs and argue over minutia, you may decide to repeat the response. You should nod sympathetically and repeat the directions. "Return to your seat, please."

10. **Avoid being drawn into juvenile discussions.** It is not necessary to explain everything. Simple obvious expectations may be assumed to be common knowledge. Restate directions such as, "Take your seat, please" or "Open your book," but do not engage in lengthy drawn-out explanations. You should not permit children to draw you into a justification of an order.

11. **Ignore the behavior.** This is one of the hardest skills to master, but it is extremely powerful. For example, if Sara is in a bad mood and is trying to get on your nerves, she might open her purse and put on some make-up. She realizes that you dislike this behavior. She also realizes that you will stop class activity and fuss at her. All eyes will be on her, she will make you mad, and she will gain some of your attention. Sara may also get to say one more "smart" remark to you. You should not fall prey to Sara's web. Ignore her. She will soon realize that she cannot manipulate you, and she will put her make-up away. If a fellow student decides to bring Sara's behavior to your attention, ignore this student or say, "I know."

12. **Sighing** can be very powerful. When Toby is calling across the room and disrupting class, stop, calmly sigh, and wait. Stand ready for Toby to come to order. Raising the right eyebrow, and if necessary, the left eyebrow, may be effective. Avoid saying anything. Students will fill in the silence with a message for themselves, and they will likely assume that you are fully aware of every rule violation they have committed over the last several weeks. Sigh and wait.

13. **Anecdotal Cards** are a great way to maintain behavior records. Pass large index cards to each student, and instruct students to write their names, addresses, parents' names, and phone numbers on the cards. Collect the cards, and tell the students that the cards will be used to keep track of their progress. Every day or two flip through the cards, and list any comments that may be useful in analyzing patterns of behavior. Try to spend no more than five minutes per class. Add comments during class. When you stop class and pick up the stack of cards, students will most likely become settled. When students are talking instead of coming to order, you should pull out the index cards and begin writing. No comments should be made about the writing. Write silently until students come to order.

Writing on anecdotal cards is more desirable than writing names on the board because often a student enjoys the attention and notoriety of having his or her name displayed for all to see. Students also want to join their friends whose names are on the board. The chalk documentation is lost when the board is erased. In addition, the mystery of the silent writing on an unknown card has a sobering effect on the class.

14. The **Conference in the Hall** can be invaluable. Students of middle school age do not respond positively to public reprimand, but they almost always comply pleasantly in private. In addition, they may be able to tell you about problems that are interfering with their self-control if they do not have an audience. The best way to open a conference is to ask in a pleasant tone of voice, "Terrence, what are you doing?" The answer may reveal a great deal. By keeping these conferences short, you will not test the patience of the class while conferencing in the hall.

15. **Tickets** can be a handy item to have in the classroom closet. Purchase a roll of 1,000 tickets from an office supply store. The cost should be less than $3.00. When a large number of students are off task, pull out a roll of tickets and pass up and down the aisles of the classroom giving tickets to the students who are on task. As you hand each on-task student a ticket, say, "Write your name on the back of this ticket." Do not explain why some students are given tickets while others are not. Let students make the observations themselves and they will put themselves in order. At the end of class, draw a name, and award that student.

16. **See me after class . . .** are four words that send chills through the hearts of middle school students. For some reasons beyond the understanding of adults, students believe this to be the ultimate in torture. When a student is off task, calmly, and as privately as possible, say, "See me after class." Make a note, or put a rubber band on your wrist, to serve as a reminder to meet with the student after class.

The remainder of class the student has the prospect of the conversation hanging over his or her head. No adult understands the dread with which the student anticipates this conversation. After class, spend a moment tidying up your desk. Stroll to the door to supervise hall activity. Acknowledge the student last and take a deep breath. Sigh. Ask the student what happened. Stall and eat up the student's socializing time between classes, but try to avoid making the student tardy or interfering with your next class. The beauty of this consequence is that it is over in less than three minutes, but the student is inconvenienced. This is a strong negative consequence.

17. **Three-part forms.** Carbonless three-part message/reply forms may be purchased at office supply stores and used to send information home about behavior at school. When a problem arises, you may quickly send a note home by the student to request help from the parent. Forms vary, but be sure to date the form and file a copy to document the contact.

A sample of a note is shown on page 61.

January 26

Dear Mr. and Mrs. Jackson,

Joanna is usually so cooperative, but today she had numerous problems following the class routine. She failed to bring her homework, made negative comments to another student, left her seat to borrow paper, and drew on a desk. Please encourage her to follow the rules of our class and to return to her usual pleasant demeanor.

Sincerely,
Mrs. Smith

(Please sign and return)

18. **"Number your paper 1–10"** is a great way to make students take notice. Give students a pop quiz on behavior. Give an oral true/false or short answer quiz. Ask students questions appropriate to the latest trend in misbehavior. Do not hesitate to ask obvious questions like "When the teacher turns out the lights, students should _____."

19. **"Pick a card . . . any card"** provides a way to intervene when chronic, minor behavior problems occur. Keep a stack of cards with consequences written on them. When a student taps his or her pencil one too many times, he or she must pick a card and serve the consequence. Possible consequences are: note home, call home, lunch detention, clean desks, Night School (see page 18), time for reflection (clean bathroom mirrors), time-out, etc. Students who have a history of hostile behavior may even be permitted to remove the card they consider to be most objectionable.

20. **A defined area** is a form of time-out. Use masking tape to mark the floor and define an area for a disruptive student. Make it clear that the student may not leave the defined area until given permission. (You may have to define *permission.*) The defined area may be enlarged by moving the tape out little by little until the student has regained normal movement. Do not use the masking tape to restrict the student's movement physically—the tape on the floor is merely symbolic.

21. **Changing class ninety seconds early** will help the disruptive student. This student will be escorted by a responsible student to the next class. The teacher who is receiving the student must insist that the student be settled into his or her seat before the rest of the team is dismissed. The student loses the freedom of socializing between classes, and problems are minimized by moving through the school when the halls are relatively empty.

22. **Lunch detention** is a natural consequence for using bad manners in the cafeteria. Students enjoy socializing at lunch, and you should take care not to use lunch detention with the same students day after day. Requiring students to sit by themselves at lunch allows them time to reflect on important lunch etiquette.

23. **Rephrase That** is useful for the student who has negative language that needs to be rethought, reflected upon, and rephrased. Give students the example below, and ask the student to rephrase the following examples of negative speech.

Example:	
Negative speech	**Positive Speech**
This is stupid.	_____
This is dumb.	_____
Man, this ain't right.	_____
You better tell him to get back.	_____
She is a geek.	_____
I am not doing that assignment.	_____
I didn't do anything.	_____
He is ugly.	_____
Give me some paper.	_____
I don't care!	_____

24. **Lighten Up** is a strategy for the student who has items that are causing distraction. The student is instructed to put all toys, gadgets, junk food, grooming aids, spray bottles, etc., into a box which is locked up for the day. The student travels lightly for the day. By paring down these unnecessary items, distractions are minimized.

25. **The Complaint Department** is for the student who tries to monopolize your time by complaining. When the student comes to you with a complaint, you may suggest that the student file a complaint. If the student does not feel strongly enough to put it in writing, he or she may drop the complaint. If complaining and arguing continue, offer the student the form for the formal complaint. The form on the following page is an example of a complaint form.

FORMAL COMPLAINT

Name _____ Date _____ Time _____

Define the nature of the complaint. _____

_____

Date and time of incident: _____

Name all people in the room during the incident. _____

_____

Describe the problem in detail. _____

_____

_____

_____

Give ten reasonable solutions to the problem and evaluate the pros and cons of each solution.

Solutions	Pros	Cons
1.		
2.		
3.		
4.		
5.		
6.		
7.		
8.		
9.		
10.		

On a scale of 1 to 10, rate the problem in terms of importance. A broken
pencil sharpener would receive a rating of 1 and a dangerous fire would get a rating of 10. _____

Explain why the problem received the above rating. _____

_____

_____

_____

_____

BEHAVIOR IMPROVEMENT PLAN

This section is to be completed by the referring teacher or principal.

Student Name _____

Referring Teacher _____

Time the student was given this assignment _____

Time the student is to be done with this assignment _____

The behavior that lead to this intervention was _____

_____

_____

_____

_____

The student may choose to apologize to _____

_____

———— To be completed by the offending student ————

In your own words write a summary of the behavior that got you in trouble.

_____

_____

_____

_____

Write a plan below that will prevent you from getting into trouble again. You must answer these questions:

- What could you have done to prevent this problem from occurring in the first place?
- What mistakes did you make?

Write your specific plan to prevent this situation from reoccurring (this must be at least seventy-five words).

_____

_____

_____

_____

_____

_____

_____

_____

_____

_____

_____

_____

_____

_____

_____

Is there anything the teachers can do to help keep you from getting into trouble again? Do you need to be moved to another seat? Does the teacher need to call your parents? Is there a personal problem that is causing you to misbehave that the teacher could help you with?

_____

_____

_____

_____

APOLOGY

You may choose to write an apology for your behavior. You need to remember that your inappropriate behavior has affected others.

_____

_____

_____

_____

Student: This form will be kept in your record. If this behavior reoccurs you will be given a more severe punishment at that time!

TWENTY-SIX REWARDS STUDENTS ENJOY

1. Permit students to pick their own assigned seats. They are to occupy the seat until the next seating change arrangement or until their behavior dictates the need to move them.

2. Occasionally, rather than grading the students' homework, surprise the students by placing a 100 on the assignments that were complete. Tell the students that today is A+ for Effort Day.

3. When walking around the classroom, place a +5 points on the student's work if the student is behaving properly.

4. Create a menu of rewards (see page 68) and permit the student to choose a reward.

5. To reward the class, permit them to design their own test. Divide the class into small groups and assign various materials to each group. The groups will design five questions over their section. A recorder should be assigned to write the questions on the actual test.

6. To reward the class, allow them to plan a party to celebrate a week of good behavior. The party will be for fifteen minutes at the end of a class period. They are to bring all the party supplies. Permit the students to play appropriate music at the party.

7. Students who follow rules during the class period may reduce their homework assignment by two questions.

8. Students who behave during the class period may do their seat work with a friend.

9. Allow students who finish their work early to play a table game in a group area.

10. Permit students with good behavior to design a bulletin board for the classroom.

11. Permit the students to teach a portion of the lesson to the class.

12. Display the students' work. Using red pen, write *Great Job*, *Superior*, or *Perfect!* on the work.

13. Keep a cassette player with earphones in the classroom. Permit a student to listen to appropriate music.

14. Assign classroom tasks to improving students. Running errands, passing out papers, and helping with lunch money builds self-esteem.

15. Permit the students to tutor each other.

16. Students who behave during the class period may write their name on a slip of paper that will be used in a drawing. At the end of the period, collect the slips and draw out a winning name. The winner receives a small reward.

17. Distribute five tokens to each student at the beginning of the class period. If a student breaks a classroom rule, take a token. The number of tokens that a student keeps is the number of bonus points the student has earned.

18. Determine a set number of minutes that the class can earn as free time at the end of the period. (Five minutes is usually appropriate.) Using a stop watch, each time the class misbehaves, start the watch. Stop it when the class settles down. Tell the class how many seconds/minutes they lost of their free time. Make certain the students see the stop watch being used. It will serve as a prompt for good behavior.

19. Place the agenda for the class period on the board. Ask on-task students to select which task they would like to do next.

20. Have a soft drink break. The last ten minutes of a class period, permit the class to go to the drink machine and purchase a soft drink. Plan this event in advance so the students will have drink money.

21. Permit cooperative students to leave class one or two minutes early. Insist that they be quiet in the hallways.

22. Send a positive note home with an improving student. Describe, in detail, how proud the parents should be of their child. Never underestimate the power of pretty paper.

23. Pat students on the back when they have been doing well.

24. Verbally praise students. Be positive and very specific with the praise.

25. Establish eye contact with a student and give him or her a smile!

26. Enjoy five minutes of peace and quiet by announcing this reward. Inform the students that they may pass notes for five minutes without talking. This encourages writing and being quiet, but the students think they are really getting away with something.

CELEBRATE!

Your behavior has been so sensational that
you may choose a reward
from the menu below:

MENU

1. Five bonus points added to your
    lowest test score.

2. Skip one test question.

3. A note sent to your family about
    your outstanding behavior.

4. A free soft drink from the
    vending machine.

5. A free ticket to an upcoming
    school event.

MANAGING HANDS-ON LESSONS

Conducting experiments, using manipulatives, and working with physical models are essential components of the effective classroom. Hands-on lessons assist the students in understanding concepts while giving them concrete objects to talk about and use. Active, hands-on learning has been proven to raise scores on standardized tests, assist students in applying new concepts, and enhance discussion in the classroom.

Some teachers are hesitant to embrace this powerful teaching method. The main reason for the hesitation is classroom management. Many teachers have seen manipulatives thrown in the classroom, equipment destroyed, and their own nerves frazzled. Usually the problem lies in the lack of preparation that must occur before a hands-on lesson is attempted. The three main areas to investigate before beginning are the following:

1. What equipment should be used?

2. How will the materials be managed?

3. What classroom rules should be reinforced or altered?

1. What equipment should be used?

Most textbook companies do a good job of recommending hands-on lesson ideas in the teacher's portion of the book. If inexperienced with hands-on learning, look over the suggestions in the textbook and choose a very simple idea. The rationale for beginning small is twofold. First, the students need to be oriented to the use of manipulatives. Second, if the idea is simple, it is more likely to be successful. When beginning, remember the adage . . . less is more!

2. How will the materials be managed?

Managing the materials is essential for a successful lesson. First, you must be experienced with the equipment. If the lesson involves pattern blocks, you need to evaluate how many blocks will be needed, how many different types of blocks there are in a set, and how manipulatives should be presented to the students.

To insure success, organize the manipulatives according to use. Using reclosable bags is a tried and true technique. If the activity is an individual activity, small size bags would be used. If organizing materials for cooperative learning, large bags would be best. Place all equipment for the lesson in the bags. It is even wise to include pencils, scrap paper, scissors, glue, or calculators. Including this equipment prevents you from being distracted by an unprepared student. If the bag has several items in it, an inventory list is an essential part of the bag. On an index card list the materials and the quantity included. When the students are cleaning up, one student may be assigned to take inventory of their reclosable bag.

Another advantage of organizing the materials into reclosable bags is in the distribution of the materials. If the students are engaged in individual activities, distribute the material by placing the bags on each student's desk. If it is a cooperative activity, place a large reclosable bag in the center of the group area. If equipment is too large for a bag, one student in each group or row may be allowed to be the materials manager. This student's responsibility is to distribute and retrieve the equipment.

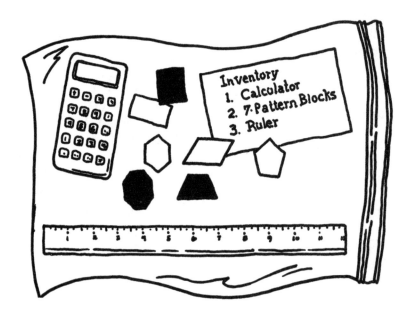

Common mistakes that occur in the management of hands-on learning are:

- You are not comfortable with the equipment.
  This situation can be avoided by your doing the lesson beforehand to pinpoint any pitfalls that the student may encounter.

- The students' behavior is unmanageable.
  To avoid discipline problems discuss appropriate behavior before the lesson begins. Discuss how the materials are to be used, how the materials will be distributed, and what the punishment will be if equipment is broken due to mishandling. It is often a good idea to allow the students a few minutes of unstructured time to "play" with the material. This takes a little bit of the newness off the materials and the students can then focus on the concepts of the lesson. The teacher must remember that he or she can always put the equipment away if behavior gets out of hand.

- Materials get stolen.

  Generally this occurs because there was not an acceptable amount of clean-up time. When using hands-on lessons, stop the lesson ten minutes before the end of the class period. The students should place all the items back in the reclosable bag. The inventory list of materials should be checked and large equipment should be brought to a central location. If calculators, hand-held microscopes, rulers, compasses, etc. were used, they must be counted. You must always know how many items were in the classroom when the students entered the class and must insist that no one is dismissed until all items are back in your possession.

3. What classroom rules should be reinforced or altered?

Rules vary from classroom to classroom, so it is difficult to write specific rules for the class during a hands-on lesson. Suggestions could include the following:

- Establish a symbol for silence. Many times students become excited about the lesson, and it is difficult to gain their attention. Blinking the lights usually is a good prompt.

- Reinforce where the students should be in the classroom. Remaining at their desks or with their group is critical.

- Reinforce proper behavior. Award bonus points for students who are acting appropriately.

- Deal quickly with anyone who is not following the rules. Isolating the student from the lesson is usually very effective.

Don't deny students the opportunity to participate in hands-on learning experiences. With planning and a strong classroom structure these activities can be enjoyable for all.

THE DREADED CLIPBOARD

The pen is mightier than the sword.

(Much mightier than the paddle.)

Try a simple experiment the next time your students are not behaving as expected. Glance at the clock. Without a word, pick up a clipboard and begin writing names and behaviors. Do not explain what you are writing.

Students become concerned about what you are writing. At first, more mature, self-controlled students will observe you writing and determine the best thing to do is to lower the profile of their behavior. They will return to their seats, become very quiet, and if you are still writing, they will take out materials and books. They will continue to model positive behaviors, and the less mature students will be a few seconds behind. You should continue to glance at the clock and to make notes.

Using the clipboard to make notes on student behavior will be a very powerful tool for behavior modification. The clipboard should go on field trips and to assemblies and be flashed when there is a guest speaker. When students are misbehaving, you can look directly at the student who is disrupting, make a note, and look back at your student. Usually, the student will make an attempt at a silent apology and will change the behavior that is causing the disturbance.

The clipboard does not have to have a stated purpose. The clipboard eliminates the need to call any student by name, thereby avoiding the complaint that others were also talking (out of their seats, brushing hair, etc.). Students generally assume that their offense is the one you observed and that they are the student whom you are writing about. Students do not need to know what you will do with the information on the clipboard. If students assume that the principal regularly reviews the clipboard or that parents are notified of every third offense, so be it. Leave the students to ponder the mystery of the clipboard.

It is possible to use the clipboard in a formal and intentional manner. The following form may prove useful in documenting behavior and making you aware of which students are actually most disruptive, but the primary use of the clipboard is prevention. At the sight of a clipboard, middle school students have been known to leave the scene of a fight where they were cheering and jeering and retreat to their assigned classroom, dash to their seats, and begin reading a glossary.

CLIPBOARD CHART

OOS = Out of seat • T = Talking • TDY = Tardy • NP = Not Participating • NFD = Not following directions

	Name	Date	Date	Date	Date	Date	Date	Date	Date
1									
2									
3									
4									
5									
6									
7									
8									
9									
10									
11									
12									
13									
14									
15									
16									
17									
18									
19									
20									
21									
22									
23									
24									
25									
26									
27									
28									
29									
30									

PARTIES AND REWARDS

Strangely enough, some students will behave beautifully in order to earn a reward, but they sabotage themselves when they receive it. This leaves teachers bewildered and annoyed. Do not give in to the temptation to forgo these powerful motivating tools because of student misbehavior. Consider having an additional motivating tool.

If there are students with a history of disrupting parties, draw them aside and tell them how much it means for them to be able to participate in the rewards that the class is earning. Explain the disappointment in their last performance and that there is concern about their behavior and self-control. Before students are invited to participate in another party, insist that they be able to pass the Party Participation Quiz on page 75. Give students this quiz, and then have an encouraging discussion with them individually or as a group. Discuss each item and constantly express confidence in their abilities to improve. Let them know that they are accountable for using their home training and their natural intelligence to assist them in their self-control. Do not permit students to participate in parties until satisfied with their completion of the quiz and their ability to participate peacefully in the class reward.

In addition, you may wish to have students sign the Party Pledge below.

I, _____,

do pledge to use my best

manners and self-control

during all class parties.

Date _____

PARTY PARTICIPATION QUIZ

Name _____ Date _____

Answer each question true or false.

_____ I have had success controlling myself at parties.

_____ Principals and teachers are responsible for making parties safe.

_____ Students and parents are responsible for making parties safe.

_____ Many hours of hard work go into making a party safe and fun.

_____ I should not show respect for adults at a party.

_____ When adults ask for my cooperation, I should respond quickly.

_____ Parties are a time to relax and have fun.

_____ Parties are a time to do dangerous and foolish things.

_____ Parties are a time to remember manners and rules.

_____ Parties are a time to be with friends.

_____ When I follow rules, I am showing maturity and intelligence.

_____ I am mature and intelligent.

_____ Students have a right to a safe and orderly environment at school (even at parties).

_____ Students have a right to ruin a party for other students.

_____ Name six reasons for behaving politely at a party. Use the back of this sheet.

GUEST SPEAKERS

There is a disturbing trend on television for audiences to be loud, rowdy, rude, and silly. There are talk shows and musical shows where the audience is even expected to be abusive to guests and performers. Students are bound to be confused about what is expected of them in their audience participation.

Many schools work as a unit in teaching audience behavior expectations to students by carefully planning assemblies from the first week of school.

Hold a practice before the first assembly. Have students practice filing in and taking their seats. Speak to students about simple expectations, keeping remarks short, positive, and encouraging. Practice polite applause, standing for the pledge to the flag, and sitting. Show them what listening looks like. Show what ignoring distraction looks like. Praise them for their success and patience. Explain that students may have to wait and that they are expected to do so patiently. If possible, hold a friendly competition between teams or classes every class can win. Winning classes may earn points toward a popcorn party or praise over the public address.

Design the first assembly to have a serious tone. This will permit the faculty to loosen the reins at a subsequent pep rally after establishing that assemblies will vary in tone and expectation. It is very difficult to go from screaming to quiet listening, but the reverse is realistic. Start seriously and move to a lively celebration.

During assemblies, students at our school are expected to:

- Pay attention to the changes in activities in the assembly

- Sit in an alert position

- Participate in polite applause and hand raising

- Avoid gum, candy, food, and drink in assemblies even though they are allowed at sports events

- Be quiet and ignore distractions

- Sit where teachers have directed

The Assembly Pledge on page 78 is another strategy you can use to remind the students of good behavior during an assembly.

ASSEMBLY PARTICIPATION QUIZ

Name _____ Date _____

Answer each question true or false.

_____ I generally control myself at assemblies.

_____ Principals and teachers are responsible for making assemblies meaningful and enjoyable.

_____ Students and parents are responsible for making assemblies meaningful and enjoyable.

_____ Many hours of hard work go into making assemblies meaningful and enjoyable.

_____ I should not show respect for performers and speakers at an assembly.

_____ When adults ask for my cooperation, I should respond quickly.

_____ Assemblies are a time to learn.

_____ Assemblies are a time to do embarrassing things.

_____ Assemblies are a time to remember manners and rules.

_____ Assemblies are a time to be with friends.

_____ When I follow rules, I am showing respect and interest.

_____ I am respectful and interested.

_____ Students have a right to listen and learn at an assembly.

_____ Students have a right to ruin an assembly for other students.

_____ Name six reasons for behaving respectfully at an assembly. Use the back of this sheet if necessary.

Positive Classroom Management _____ 77

ASSEMBLY PLEDGE

We, the undersigned, agree to show courtesy to all speakers, to follow the directions of assembly leaders, to encourage all student leaders, to show proper appreciation to all performers and to uphold the standards of our school's reputation as a center of art and learning.

Using Literature & Drama to Impact Student Behavior

THE BOOK OF VIRTUES

Edited, with Commentary by William J. Bennett

In 1993, William J. Bennett, former Secretary of Education, compiled hundreds of stories that help children develop character. His collection includes philosophy from Plato, Bible stories, selections from Martin Luther King, Jr., fairy tales, and numerous other selections. Mr. Bennett had hoped that families would read this book together. He believed that this book would help the family learn and enjoy one another.

This book is also a wonderful tool for teachers. With chapters on self-discipline, responsibility, work, and honesty, William Bennett has created a great foundation for teachers to use as a springboard to better classroom behavior. Any of the stories could be read and used for a group discussion on virtue and character. For example, if the teacher is dealing with a classwide problem with compassion, he or she might select "The Beauty and the Beast" or "The Little Match Girl."

Another way to use this book is to use specific stories as intervention for misbehaving students. Rather than send a student to the office or assign the student meaningless tasks, remove *The Book of Virtues* from the shelf and assign a particular reading assignment.

The following pages are examples of written assignments based on selections from *The Book of Virtues*. The assignments contain two parts. The first part, Gathering Information, contains questions that relate to the content of the story or poem. The second part of the written assignment, Personal Application, asks the student to use the story or poem to evaluate the behavior that got him or her in trouble. Using this type of intervention allows the student to think about his or her inappropriate behavior while reading good literature.

REBECCA

by Hilaire Belloc

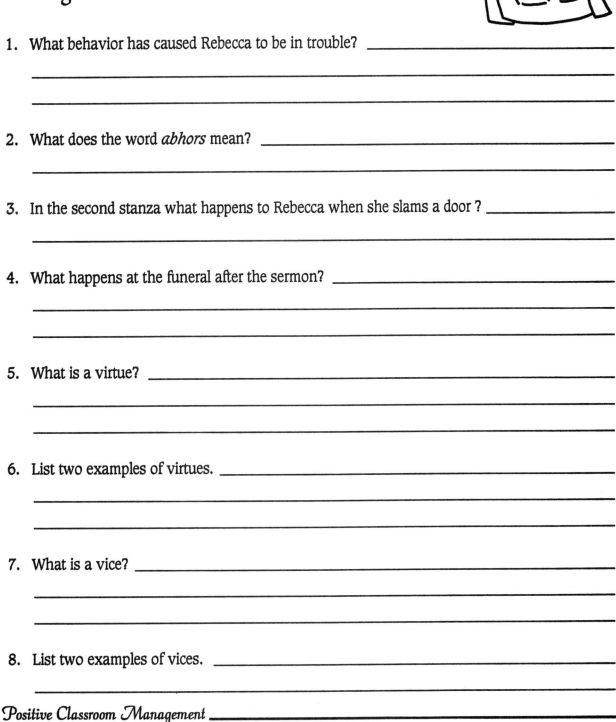

Read the poem "Rebecca" by Hilaire Belloc and then answer the following questions.

Gathering Information

1. What behavior has caused Rebecca to be in trouble? _____
   _____
   _____

2. What does the word *abhors* mean? _____
   _____

3. In the second stanza what happens to Rebecca when she slams a door ? _____
   _____

4. What happens at the funeral after the sermon? _____
   _____
   _____

5. What is a virtue? _____
   _____
   _____

6. List two examples of virtues. _____
   _____
   _____

7. What is a vice? _____
   _____
   _____

8. List two examples of vices. _____
   _____

9. At the funeral does the sermon dwell on Rebecca's virtues or her vices? _____

_____

10. What do the children at the funeral decide? _____

_____

_____

Personal Application

11. What behavior has caused you to be in trouble? _____

_____

_____

_____

12. Why does your teacher think your behavior is dangerous? What could happen to you or
    others? _____

_____

_____

_____

13. Do you believe that your teacher is being reasonable or unreasonable about his or her
    concern for you or others? _____

_____

_____

_____

_____

14. Write a plan to stop the behavior that is getting you into trouble. _____

_____

_____

_____

_____

_____

_____

THE KING AND HIS HAWK

Retold by James Baldwin

Read the story "The King and His Hawk" and answer the following questions.

Gathering Information

1. Describe Genghis Khan in twenty-five words or less. _____

_____

_____

_____

2. What sits on Genghis Khan's wrist? _____

3. What does Genghis Khan need to satisfy? _____

4. What does he find to fulfill the need? _____

5. Describe the behavior of the hawk. _____

_____

_____

_____

6. Describe Genghis Khan's response to the hawk.

_____

_____

_____

_____

7. What was the hawk trying to tell Genghis Khan?

_____

_____

_____

_____

8. What did Genghis Khan learn that day? _____

_____

_____

Personal Application

9. Describe how anger has gotten you into trouble. _____

_____

_____

_____

_____

10. Have you ever found ways to control your behavior? If so, list them below. _____

_____

_____

_____

_____

11. What can others do to help you control your anger? _____

_____

_____

_____

12. Write a plan below that will help you control your anger next time you feel yourself losing control. _____

_____

_____

_____

_____

_____

_____

_____

DIAMONDS AND TOADS

Retold by Charles Perrault

Read the story "Diamonds and Toads"
and answer the following questions.

Gathering Information

1. Name and describe the four main characters in the story.

   _____

   _____

   _____

   _____

2. What task is the younger daughter expected to perform twice a day? _____

   _____

   _____

3. Who does the younger daughter find at the spring? _____

   _____

   _____

4. Describe the younger daughter's behavior at the spring. _____

   _____

   _____

   _____

   _____

   _____

5. What good fortune comes upon the younger daughter? Why does this happen to her?

   _____

   _____

   _____

   _____

6. When the younger daughter comes home, what does the mother decide to do that involves the elder daughter? _____

_____

_____

7. Does the elder daughter want to obey her mother? _____

_____

_____

8. Describe what happens to the elder daughter at the spring. _____

_____

_____

Personal Application

9. What rude behavior has caused you to be in trouble? _____

_____

_____

10. Was your behavior similar to the behavior of the elder daughter? How or how not? _____

_____

_____

_____

11. Write at least two ways that rude behavior causes you to be in trouble. _____

_____

_____

_____

12. Write your plan for stopping your rude behavior. _____

_____

_____

_____

_____

_____

THE ROAD NOT TAKEN

by Robert Frost

Read the poem "The Road Not Taken" and answer the following questions.

Gathering Information

1. How many roads went into a yellow wood? _____

2. Did the traveler know at first which road to take? _____

3. Describe the second road.

   _____
   _____
   _____
   _____

4. Which road did the traveler take? _____

Personal Application

5. How could this poem relate to you? _____

   _____
   _____
   _____
   _____
   _____

6. What do you think the poet meant by the lines, "I took the one less traveled by, And that has made all the difference"? _____

   _____
   _____
   _____
   _____

7. Write about a time when you followed the crowd and you got into trouble because of it.

_____

_____

_____

_____

_____

_____

_____

8. Write about a time when you went against what others wanted you to do and it turned out better for you. _____

_____

_____

_____

_____

_____

_____

9. If a friend came to you and told you that all his buddies were wanting him to steal something from the store in order to be in their group, what would you tell him? _____

_____

_____

_____

_____

_____

10. Write three things you could say to someone if he or she were trying to convince you to do something that you knew was not right.

1. _____

_____

2. _____

_____

3. _____

_____

THE HONEST WOODMAN

Adapted from Emilie Poulsson

Read the story "The Honest Woodman" and answer the following questions.

Gathering Information

1. The Woodman believes that as long as he has _____ ,
   he can take care of his family.

2. How does he lose his axe? Where does it land? _____

   _____

   _____

   _____

   _____

   _____

3. Who appears before the Woodman? _____

4. What does the fairy first show the Woodman and
   what does he tell her? _____

   _____

   _____

   _____

   _____

5. What does the fairy show the Woodman the second
   time? What does he tell her? _____

   _____

   _____

   _____

   _____

6. What does the fairy show the Woodman the third time? What does he tell her? _____

_____

_____

_____

7. What is the Woodman's reward for his honesty? _____

_____

_____

_____

_____

Personal Application

8. Do you think it was easy for the Woodman to tell the truth about his axe? Why or why not?

_____

_____

_____

_____

_____

_____

_____

_____

_____

9. Pretend the Woodman was able to tell the fairy that the silver axe wasn't his, but he lied and told her that the golden axe did belong to him. In the space below write how the story would have turned out with this new twist. _____

_____

_____

_____

_____

_____

10. Describe how lying has caused you to be in trouble. _____

_____

_____

_____

_____

11. What do you think would have been the "worst" thing that would have happened to you if you told the truth instead of lying? _____

_____

_____

12. Write a paragraph to yourself that you are going to try to remember before you think about lying again.

_____

_____

_____

_____

_____

13. Do you want to be trusted by others, or do you want to be known as a liar? _____

_____

_____

_____

_____

ECLECTIC TRAGIC BEHAVIOR OPERA

The following spoof may be performed by students or brave teachers to illustrate the folly of disruptive behavior. The melodies are easily accessible, including the two operatic melodies, but teachers may change the tunes to suit the needs and abilities of the present performers.

Characters: Miss Pacific — a calm, caring teacher
                Figaro — a disruptive student
                Chorus — any number of Figaro's classmates in any off-beat apparel from any era

Miss Pacific stands in front of her class in an operatic gown and a lab coat preparing to show her class a beaker of baking soda and another of vinegar.

(Sung to the tune "My Bonnie")

Chorus: Our class has been studying chemistry.
           Our class has been busy as bees.
           Our class has been studying chemistry
           Oh, bring on that chemistry!
           Bring on!
           Bring on!
           Oh bring on that happenin' chemistry!
           Bring on,
           Oh bring on,
           Oh, bring on that chemistry.

(Sung to the tune "Some Enchanted Evening.")

Miss Pacific: Here inside my classroom
                I have such good children.
                I have such good children
                Except for just a few.
                That here in the lab
                I'm able to show
                How Bunsen Burners ignite in a glow.

                Here inside my classroom
                I have such good students
                Wonderful students
                I know they will follow
                All of my directions
                And so I will show
                All of the wonderful things that I know.

                Once they have settled, I'll show what I know.
                Once they have settled, I'll show what I know.

(Turns and prepares to combine baking soda and vinegar)

Figaro: **(Breaks a pencil and throws it across the room.)**

(Sung to the tune of "Figaro!" This tune uses the notes E, D, and C.)

Miss Pacific: Figaro!
Figaro, Figaro, Figaro!

Figaro: **(Spoken rudely.)** Yeah!

Miss Pacific: Figaro!
Figaro, Figaro, Figaro

Figaro: **(Spoken.)** What?

(Sung to the tune "Yankee Doodle.")

Miss Pacific: Throwing pencils, breaking crayons,
Never having Science books!
Hitting girls and spitting wads
And sleeping during class, gadzooks!

(Sung to the tune "My Bonnie.")

Chorus: **(With concern and sincerity.)**
Our class needs to learn and to practice.
Our class needs to work, play, and grow.
Our class needs to find a solution.

(With determination.)
Our class should get rid of Figaro!
Get lost!
Get lost!
Oh, beat it, old Figaro,
You're such a clown.
Get lost!
Oh, get lost.
We can't learn when you are around.

Miss Pacific: **(Spoken.)** Figaro, I am afraid I have to agree with the class. It is not safe to conduct an experiment with objects flying across the room.

Figaro: **(Dejected, goes out to stand in the hall.)**

Miss Pacific: **(With flourish pours vinegar into beaker with baking soda.)**

Chorus: **(Gasps with delight. Applauds.)**

Figaro: **(Hears applause and delightful gasping from hall. Winces with regret.)**

Chorus and Miss Pacific:	**(Pantomime preparations for individual experiments.)**
Figaro:	**(Dashes to locker and dons a disguise. Walks back into class in disguise and crosses to Miss Pacific.)** Hello. My name is Hamlet Macbeth, a new student from Glasgow, Denmark.
Miss Pacific:	**(Delighted.)** Hamlet, we are glad to have you here with us at La Scala Middle School. Have a seat and we will continue our investigation.
Figaro:	**(Aside. Sung to the melody of the March from "Aida" or with slight adjustments, "Twist and Shout.")** Oh, I, I have been throwing paper wads all my life First grade Third grade Seventh grade. And now, I have seen how my mischief destroys the environment The trees The rain forest This class. **(Crosses to Miss Pacific. Drops to one knee. Removes disguise.)** Oh, please. Please forgive me. I have been wasteful Mischievous, Fraudulent, And a cad. Alas! If I have one more chance You'll see how I'll change. And you'll have a student who obeys. **(To chorus.)** I'll learn. I will study every night and I'll try To learn, To study, To prepare.
Chorus:	**(Rises as march finishes and marches past Figaro, congratulating him.)**
Miss Pacific and Figaro:	**(Sung to the "Theme of the Andy Griffith Television Show.")** Oh it's fine now to have some fun To cut up when your work is done. Oh it's great so don't hesitate. Go for it if you're done. **(Whistle.)** When it's all done.

(Whistle.)
When it's all done.

(Whistle.)
When it's all done.
You cut up when it's done.
With your books, and your homework you
Are ready to be good as new.
So behave and we'll start again
And you'll have great new friends.

Chorus: **(Whistle.)**
Start again.

(Whistle.)
Start again.

(Whistle.)
Start again.
And you'll have great new friends.

All: So if you want to have the tools,
You follow classroom rules.
Wow!

Dealing with Difficult Students and Situations

ASSISTING THE STUDENT
WHO IS IN DANGER OF FAILING

This letter can be sent to parents to warn them of their child's lack of progress. Deborah Broyles at Two Rivers Middle School sends an adaptation of the following letter to the parents of her students.

Date _____

Dear Parents or Guardian,

Help your child succeed! Your involvement can change the direction of your child's education. We are confident that your child can improve, but this letter is to inform you of your child's lack of academic progress. Your child is failing or is in danger of failing the following subjects:

Subject	Average	Teacher's Name
____ Language Arts	_____	_____
____ Social Studies	_____	_____
____ Science	_____	_____
____ Math	_____	_____

Below are suggestions that will assist your child in improving his or her academic progress:

- Schedule a conference with your child's team of teachers (_____-_____).
- Request progress reports from the teachers. Make your child aware that you are checking on his or her academic progress.
- Communicate with your child about class and homework assignments.
- Watch for and inquire about textbooks, subject area notebooks, and school supplies.
- Consistently praise your child's effort.
- Establish small rewards for short term goals. For example, a good progress report could earn the child the privilege of having a friend come for a sleepover on Friday night.
- Be firm with the child. Expect improvement. Clearly state your expectations.
- Teach your child the meaning of responsibility. He or she must be responsible for his or her actions.
- Use great motivating tactics like homework contracts.

Remember, the best schools are the ones which have the support of the families they serve. The teachers, the administration, and the guidance counselor are willing to assist you with your child's progress.

Sincerely,

Please sign and return this letter by _____ .

Signature _____ Date _____

ASSISTING THE STUDENT
WHO WILL FAIL

As soon as it becomes apparent that a student will not be promoted to the next grade, you should notify the parents immediately. The parents must be aware of support services that the child can receive. There may be other helpful strategies that the parents can use. The letter below could be sent to a parent when this situation arises.

Date _____

Dear Parents or Guardian,

As you know from report cards and progress reports, your child has shown marginal progress in meeting the requirements for passing to the next grade. While it is natural to feel discouraged at this time, this may prove to be an opportunity for your child to learn skills and habits which will prove valuable throughout high school and beyond.

Most students in this position are eligible to attend summer school. In addition, you may choose to use trips and vacations for providing visits to museums and libraries. The public library has a reading program and story hours for students of all ages. Every time you show your child how to manage money, use measurement, calculate mileage, or estimate the cost of a shopping list, you are assisting him or her in mathematics. Although these activities are important, the most important thing to demonstrate to your child is your love.

In order to attend summer school, your child will need to register and complete some paperwork. Please call the school office and we will assist you.

Other options to consider are private tutoring and academic camps. Schedule a conference with the school staff, and we will help you find the best strategy for your child. It may be that with hard work your child can go to the next grade in the fall. It will take all of us working together to achieve this important goal.

Sincerely,

ASSISTING THE STUDENT WHO IS ANGRY

Teachers recognize that much of students' misbehavior stems from their inability to handle anger. Teachers are generally not trained to assist students with deep, underlying problems that are affecting them at school. Hopefully, guidance counselors, psychologists, and school nurses are standing ready to give support and advice to the students and teachers who need help. However, in this day of budget cuts and returning to basics, teachers may be the only support students have at school.

When you encounter problems with an angry student, discuss various strategies with him or her, including the tips below. The student may choose to carry these tips on a laminated card with him or her at all times.

In order to increase the student's awareness of anger management strategies and to assess student progress, you may use the **Self-Assessment in Anger Management** questionnaire found on page 101.

TAKING CHARGE OF YOUR ANGER!
- Count to ten before you speak or act.
- Decide exactly what you are angry about.
- Choose the person who needs to hear your complaint.
- Explore possible courses of action.
- Practice your speech.
- Examine the consequences of your actions or words.
- Choose your course of action.
- Choose your words.
- Take action.

After meeting with the student and working on anger management, you may wish to ask other teachers to share their observations. Give them the **Teacher Assessment in Anger Management Survey** included on page 102. By periodically collecting the data from the questionnaires on the following pages, parents, counselors, and teachers will gain a more accurate picture of the student's progress.

SELF-ASSESSMENT IN ANGER MANAGEMENT

Self-assessment is a major tool in personal growth. Circle the word in each statement that describes your actions.

1. I realize the signs that let me know that I am beginning to get angry.

    never   sometimes   often   usually   almost always

2. I am using the techniques that assist me to gain control over my anger.

    never   sometimes   often   usually   almost always

3. I remember the importance of safety, security, and an orderly environment at school.

    never   sometimes   often   usually   almost always

4. I remember that I can walk away from the situation that is causing me to lose control.

    never   sometimes   often   usually   almost always

5. When I am feeling angry I remember the negative consequences that losing my temper will cause.

    never   sometimes   often   usually   almost always

6. On a scale of 1–5 (1 = very unsuccessful and 5 = very successful), rate how you have done this week controlling your anger._____

7. Write a paragraph about a time this week when you were able to control your anger.

_____

_____

_____

_____

_____

_____

_____

_____

_____

_____

TEACHER ASSESSMENT IN ANGER MANAGEMENT

Assessment is a major tool in personal growth. Circle the word in each statement that describes the behaviors you have noticed about _____ and his or her progress in anger management.

1. I realize that the student is aware of the signs that let him or her know that he or she is beginning to get angry.

    never   sometimes   often   usually   almost always

2. I have observed the student using techniques that assist him or her to gain control over the anger.

    never   sometimes   often   usually   almost always

3. The student seems to be aware of the importance of safety, security, and an orderly environment at school.

    never   sometimes   often   usually   almost always

4. The student has removed himself or herself from situations that could cause the loss of self-control.

    never   sometimes   often   usually   almost always

5. The student seems to be aware of the negative consequences that losing control will cause.

    never   sometimes   often   usually   almost always

6. On a scale of 1–5 (1 = very unsuccessful and 5 = very successful), rate how the student has done this week controlling anger. _____

7. Write any observations you have about the student and his or her ability to control anger.

_____ *Positive Classroom Management*

ASSISTING THE STUDENT WHO DOES NOT PARTICIPATE

Many teachers include participation as a part of the grade. This helps many students, but there are some students who do not demonstrate participation behaviors in the classroom. Perhaps no one has ever shared with the students what behaviors demonstrate active participation. Before making participation a part of a grade, spend time informing the students what behaviors will be considered. It is also important to describe ways that will raise the quality of participation. The checklist below is designed to take the mystery out of participation grades and to give students feedback regarding observable behaviors.

Self-Evaluation of Participation

Name _____ Date _____

Rank yourself on participation behaviors.
The scale is   3 = Excellent   2= Good   1= Fair   0= Needs improvement

Behavior	Mon.	Tues.	Wed.	Thurs.	Fri.
Attends class					
Arrives on time					
Has materials in class					
Raises hand					
Asks questions					
Listens to others					
Maintains eye contact					
Takes notes					
Encourages others to participate					
Ignores distractions					
Avoids interrupting					
Writes down assignments					
Completes homework					
Turns in work					
Maintains alert posture					
Answers questions					

ASSISTING THE STUDENT WHO IS HOSTILE

One of the most unpleasant and stressful problems for teachers is maintaining a positive classroom climate when the class contains students who are hostile. These students should be separated from each other as much as possible. Encourage their interaction with students who have shown positive leadership. Cooperative learning activities will assist these students in resigning their hostile behaviors.

Practice superhuman self-control with these students. A teacher will never win a test of wills with a student who is exhibiting hostile behavior. Ignoring rude and hostile behavior is by far the most powerful and effective method for eradicating animosity. Remember that even when their anger and reluctance has nothing to do with the educational environment, these students try to push everyone's buttons and make it personal. These comments and actions are best ignored or discussed in private.

Some hostility is normal adolescent confusion, and it is probably going to fade as the student builds a rapport with others. Unfortunately, some hostility is a result of any number of circumstances and cannot be erased. You need to do everything possible to assist this student and keep the class running. With hostile behavior, document the subtle, repeated problems, and look for patterns. Every avenue of friendship and openness must be explored with these students, yet at the same time careful documentation must be maintained.

The following checklist may be helpful in keeping track of progress. A team of teachers may use this checklist to document behavior. Be sure to date the checklists in order to analyze changes in behavior patterns. Also look at the times of day that most problems occur and the times that are most successful for the student.

When the student resists discussion of problems, use the letter on page 107 to open a dialogue to help the student.

STUDENT BEHAVIOR ASSESSMENT

Date _____

Dear Colleagues,

Please fill out the following checklist on _____
and return it to _____ . Check all that apply to your
general experience with this student as compared to the rest of your class. This assessment will
help determine positive behaviors that the student is exhibiting. Any behavior that is not checked
will be seen as a behavior that the student needs to acquire.

Person making observation _____

- ☐ 1. Arrives in class on time
- ☐ 2. Is prepared for class
- ☐ 3. Will communicate regarding needed materials
- ☐ 4. If not prepared, will accept materials
- ☐ 5. Will use materials brought or accepted
- ☐ 6. Takes materials out to prepare for class
- ☐ 7. Opens book when instructions are given
- ☐ 8. Sits up in seat
- ☐ 9. Opens book and prepares for class
- ☐ 10. Appears to pay attention
- ☐ 11. Follows directions given to the class
- ☐ 12. Follows individual directions
- ☐ 13. Speaks clearly and understandably
- ☐ 14. Asks questions
- ☐ 15. Appears to follow the class activity
- ☐ 16. Attempts assignments
- ☐ 17. Turns in assignments as directed
- ☐ 18. Participates in cooperative group activities
- ☐ 19. Interacts positively with classmates
- ☐ 20. Uses appropriate language
- ☐ 21. Speaks respectfully to adults when answering
- ☐ 22. Allows others in class to participate
- ☐ 23. Follows class routine for cleaning up
- ☐ 24. Follows class routine for turning in assignments

☐ 25. Follows class routine for dismissal

☐ 26. Uses class materials carefully

☐ 27. Leaves furniture, walls, books, and materials clean

☐ 28. Keeps hands, feet, and objects to self

☐ 29. Shows interest in class activity

☐ 30. Shows effort in assignments

☐ 31. Uses pleasant facial expressions

☐ 32. Becomes compliant when corrected

☐ 33. Makes polite requests

☐ 34. Is patient with mistakes of others

☐ 35. Is patient with own mistakes

☐ 36. When instructed to change activity, changes smoothly

☐ 37. When accidents occur, makes changes calmly

☐ 38. When other students are disruptive, can ignore distractions

☐ 39. Expects reasonable amount of attention

☐ 40. Is patient when waiting

☐ 41. Accepts suggestions from others

☐ 42. Remains in assigned area

☐ 43. Handles manipulatives appropriately

☐ 44. Encourages others to participate and to follow directions

☐ 45. Shows respect for teacher

☐ 46. Shows respect for peers

☐ Other (Please add any comments that add to an accurate picture of this student.)

_____

_____

_____

_____

_____

_____

_____

_____

_____

STUDENT BEHAVIOR CHECKLIST

Date _____

Dear _____ ,

You are having problems in class, and I want to help you. Please check the things you think will help you have a productive day and will help you behave so that others in the class can learn.

_____ Help understanding the instructions

_____ Help understanding the assignment

_____ Help getting organized

_____ Reminder to start working

_____ Need to move seat to the front of the room

_____ Need to move seat near the teacher's desk

_____ Need supplies (check the ones you need)

     _____ Paper

     _____ Pencil

     _____ Book

     _____ Folder

_____ Help with homework

_____ Reminders not to talk

_____ Time out when you do not follow the rules

_____ Praise when you follow the rules

Also, list your own ideas that you think would help you be more successful in school.

_____

_____

_____

_____

_____

Check two of the suggestions you think will help and we will start trying these first. If we work together, I know you can be successful, your classmates can enjoy the day, and I can help everyone in our class. Let's make it work.

Sincerely,

_____

ASSISTING THE STUDENT WHO IS UNPREPARED

Dealing with unprepared students is not usually the most hazardous situation to handle in the classroom, but an unprepared student can be very irritating and can be the cause of a great loss of instructional time. Nagging and punishing will not solve this behavior problem. It will take a proactive approach from you, the teacher.

What you can do to help the unprepared student:

1. Make it clear to the student what materials need to be brought to class. The poster on page 110 could be hung by the entrance of the classroom. Post all the necessary materials. Don't assume that the student knows he or she will always need paper and pencil. Occasionally, it may be necessary for you to stand by the sign, stop particular students, and ask them to read it.

2. When collecting homework, it is best to stand at the entrance of the classroom as the class is entering and ask the students to turn in the assignment at that time. If a student did not bring it, then before class begins the student can go get the work from his or her locker. This procedure saves valuable class time because the homework has already been turned in before the class period begins.

3. If you want students to bring a notebook everyday, one way to insure that each student has one is to make it an invaluable resource. The notebook will be invaluable if the students can use notes from the notebook on quizzes. You may want to ask the students to place page 111 in the front of the notebook. This page has valuable coupons on it. The students may redeem these in the classroom if this sheet is in their notebooks.

4. Use the middle school fascination with lockers to your advantage by making a locker poster (page 110) with reminders to bring materials to class.

5. When the student does not have the necessary materials, you must decide what the consequences will be and how much class time should be spent on this problem. Some suggestions include:

    •   If the student forgets a pencil, provide the student with a pencil and place the student's name on the board. You may choose to sell pencils. In order to prevent delaying the opening of class, a student may be assigned to sell pencils.

    •   If the student forgets a textbook, make the student share with you.

    •   If the student forgets an assignment, take off five points from the score because the assignment was late.

- If the student turns in an assignment that is only partially complete, take up the assignment anyway and grade it. The grade will reflect the consequence of not completing it.

Avoid the following actions. Students tend to enjoy these consequences:

- Going to their lockers during class time to find the forgotten assignment.

- Sharing textbooks with friends.

- Being sent to the principal to get a pencil. This enables the students to skip most of the class.

A Reminder

Today you will need the following materials for class:

1. _____

2. _____

3. _____

4. _____

5. _____

Don't **assume** you have these materials. Check to see that you have them **with you** before you enter the classroom.

You will **not** be permitted to go get them once class begins!

Notebook Coupons

Name _____

Keep this page in the front of your notebook. You may redeem these valuable coupons only if they are in your notebook and your notebook is in class with you.

These coupons are not transferable.

Name _____ ## FREE ANSWER PASS *Redeem this coupon for* the removal of one test question.	Name _____ ## A 5 POINTER *Redeem this coupon for* Five Additional Points on any Test or Quiz.
Name _____ ## A 10 POINTER *Redeem this coupon for* Ten Additional Points on any Homework Assignment.	Name _____ ## 1 DAY OF GRACE *Redeem this coupon for* a 1-day (and 1 day only) extension on any assignment.

ASSISTING THE STUDENT WHO IS TEACHER-DEPENDENT

Vignette:

Ms. Smith has just finished her portion of the lesson. She has now assigned page 34 in the textbook to her students. She monitors the students for several minutes and everyone seems to have a clear understanding of the assignment, except Larry. Ms. Smith goes over to his desk and explains the next question to Larry. She realizes that he has the basic idea, but he needed to look at a term on the previous page. Larry quickly completes his answer, and Ms. Smith notices that all the students are working on the assignment.

Larry now moves on to question 2. He reads it once and doesn't "get it," so he raises his hand. Ms. Smith comes to his desk and assists Larry. He simply needed to refer to a diagram at the bottom of the page.

Larry never attempts to help himself. His strategy is to look at the question quickly and read it one time. If he doesn't know for sure what the answer is, he summons Ms. Smith.

Ms. Smith likes Larry, but she does lose her patience with him. Larry is bright and makes good grades, yet he is constantly asking for help. She is unsure whether he just lacks self-confidence or if he lacks the knowledge to tap resources that are available in the classroom. As she thinks about him going to high school next year, she realizes she needs to help Larry become a more independent student.

A student like Larry needs help with his time-management skills. In the time it takes him to raise his hand and wait on Ms. Smith to get to him he could look in the index, ask his study partner, refer to a diagram, reread the question, reread a paragraph, or review the example in the textbook. One intervention for students like Larry is a "Seeking out Resources Checklist." A sample checklist is on page 113. Conference with the student, and ask the student to keep the checklist for a week. Each item on the checklist should be discussed with the student. Does the student understand the purpose of the glossary and index? Is the student aware of resource material available throughout the school? At the end of the week, review the strategies the student has used. At this time, set a goal that will decrease the number of times the student asks you for help and increase the number of times the student uses other resources. The goal of the intervention is to train the student to use resources other than you. The student needs to know that at times the teacher is the best resource, but not every time a question arises.

Another strategy that would assist the student is to develop a slogan that will encourage more independent behavior. Ideas for slogans could include:

- Well begun is half done.

- So many resources . . . so little time.

Seeking out Resources Checklist

Name _____

As you work on assignments, keep a
tally of how many times a day you use
resources other than your teacher. Place a
check in the box that describes the resource
you used. Each time you ask a teacher for
help, place a check in the row called "Asked a Teacher." Tally the
number of times you used resources other than a teacher. Compare
this total to the number of times you asked a teacher for help.
You should use other resources many more times than you consult
with teachers.

Resources	Date	Date	Date	Date	Date
1. Reread the assignment.					
2. Consulted the index of the textbook.					
3. Reread relevant material.					
4. Used a reference book.					
5. Asked a friend.					
6. Other					
7. Total					
8. Asked a teacher.					

ASSISTING THE STUDENT WHO IS A CONSTANT TALKER

Dealing with a student who is a constant talker is frustrating. Many times the student wants to control his or her behavior, but is unable to do so on his or her own. "Staying on the Right Path" on page 115 is an intervention that will assist the student in controlling the talking behavior. The student or the class will receive a copy of the sheet and it will be placed in a notebook. Each letter grade is divided on the page by a line. When the student talks without permission, the strip with the highest grade level will be cut off. The sheet was designed to be used for an entire week. A goal is set for the student/class that will help curb the talking behavior. A student with a severe problem will set a goal of possibly a C. Each week the goal should be refined to meet the needs of the student.

At the beginning of this intervention a letter should be sent to the parent. The letter on page 116 is an example of a parent letter that should be sent home at the beginning of this intervention.

Staying on the Right Path!

Each time you are not following the rules, the strip with the highest grade will be cut off. To consider your behavior satisfactory, you must have a grade of at least ____. On Thursday you will take this slip home and have a parent or guardian sign it.

Name_____ Date _____

Parent's Signature _____

Comments _____

_____

_____

_____

	0
	D-
	D
	D+
	C-
	C
	C+
	B-
	B
	B+
	A-
	A
	A+

STAYING ON THE RIGHT PATH

Date _____

Dear Parents,

Below is a copy of a behavior management strategy that I am using with your child. "Staying on the Right Path" is a strategy that will assist your son or daughter in controlling his or her talking. Each time a student talks without permission a grade level section will be cut off of the form. Each week a goal will be set as to what is an acceptable grade. These grades will not be averaged into a student's academic average, but will be used as an indicator of conduct at school.

Each Thursday the student will bring home the "Staying on the Right Path" sheet for you to sign and return to school. Please feel free to write comments on the form. Discuss the form with your child. Please look at the student's goal for the week. Please praise him or her if the goal was met or exceeded. Encourage your child to try harder if he or she failed to meet the goal of the week. Please call the school if you have any questions about this program.

Sincerely,

ASSISTING THE STUDENT WHO IS GRUMPY

Use this proofreading exercise to help the student assess his or her behavior.

Editor _____ Date _____

Match the following proofreading symbols with their functions.

A $\underline{\underline{a}}$ ℓ $\wedge$ $\P$ $\overset{a}{\wedge}$ $\overset{\vee}{}$ (sp)

| Indent | Add a comma | Delete (Take it out.) | Lowercase |
| Add | Add an apostrophe | Capitalize | Check the spelling |

Use proofreading symbols to edit the following paragraphs from *How to Be Grumpy* by Fumidore B. Dour. Do not change Fumidore's advice, just correct his spelling, grammar, and punctuation.

In order to be a proper grump you must get a bad nights sleep by putting rocks under your pillow and sleeping with your head on the floor Be sure to get up on the wrong side of the bed. Do not get up when you are called wait at least for the tenth time they call you

grumpes live in garbage cans, old junk cars, or even in beautiful houses Keep your room messy with old drink bottles dirty clothes and little pieces of games. if you have to straighten it up just put everything under the rug.

Wear grumpy clothes. Keep wholes in all of your clothes and don't let anyone wash them two often. Remeber that you can wear very expensive clothes if you keep them a little dirty and smelly. Let the stains set before you tell your parent about them

Eat grumpy food. Most grumpes eat sauerkraut and catsup with peanut butter. An excellent choice for desert is chunky tuna ice cream with chicken gravy.

Have grumpy days. grumpes hate warm sunny days. They love cold, rainy weather. Bad weather makes grumps happy which makes them sad. Being sad makes them hippy which makes them sad, but that makes them happy.

ASSISTING THE STUDENT WHO NEEDS AN ALTERNATIVE TO SUMMER SCHOOL

Summer Non-School

Sometimes a student's progress makes a borderline case for retention, but summer school is not available as an option for remediation or enrichment. With parent support, a teacher may choose to recommend an independent study.

The instructions beginning on page 120 were designed for Fred, a student who had not reached his potential due to behavior problems throughout the year. He seldom paid attention in class, and he was rarely prepared. He seemed too distracted by his social problems to learn, and his grades were not good enough for him to advance to the next grade.

Fred's greatest difficulty arose from his inappropriate efforts to make friends. Classmates often complained that he was staring at them and even said that he was "stalking" them. Fred made endless phone calls to students who were not interested in being his friends. He took pencils and paper from students to gain their attention, and he followed girls right to the bathroom door where they would retreat for a moment's peace. Some students in Fred's class made overtures of friendship, but his clinging behavior often made them uncomfortable. Finally the offer of friendship would be withdrawn.

Fred's parents were concerned. They had divorced three years before, and his mother lived out of state. Summer school would make a summer visit with her impossible. Fred's father was taking him to counseling and the counselor had recommended a special camp for two weeks of the summer where they hoped Fred would learn to make friends and improve his self-esteem. Summer school had not been successful for Fred even though he had attended the previous three summers. Fred's parents agreed to provide the time and resources for him to complete the assignments described below. Essentially, they were home schooling him with curricular guidance from the school.

Teachers will want to have the advice and approval of their administrators in recommending this course of action. The following letter to parents explains why this alternative may be offered. A face-to-face conference with parents, an administrator, and a guidance counselor is an excellent way to explore all possibilities.

Central Middle School
100 Main Street
Grant, TX 99999

May 2, 1997

Dear Mr. Brand,

As we have discussed, in spite of good progress in many areas, Fred's behavior continues to interfere with his learning. Ordinarily we would recommend summer school under these circumstances, but due to your unique family situation and Fred's past difficulties in summer school, we would like to offer an alternative.

I have discussed some possibilities with our principal and we agree that Fred needs some individualized instruction, but we do not want to interfere with the counseling that you and his mother are providing, nor do we want to interfere with his summer visit with his mother. Please call 555-6854 to arrange a conference. Of course we would also be delighted to speak with Fred's mother to reassure her and to answer questions regarding our recommendations for the summer and next year.

Let's work together to create a plan for Fred to encourage his academic and social progress and to insure a productive summer.

Sincerely,

Mary Pleasant

Mary E. Pleasant

Mr. Brand was most appreciative of this opportunity, and Mrs. Brand also expressed her appreciation for the school's concern and flexibility. After a conference with Fred, Mr. Brand, the team of teachers, the principal, and the guidance counselor, Ms. Pleasant agreed to consolidate everyone's ideas and to write a letter clarifying the plan. It follows.

Dear Fred,

Please complete the following tasks and turn them in to the office each week or two throughout the summer. We think the following assignments will be beneficial to you.

Science

Find one nature or science magazine each week and complete the following tasks. Try to find a variety of topics including health, environment, chemistry, biology, and energy.

- Read two articles.
- Describe the main idea of each article.
- Give two surprising facts from each article and tell why you were surprised.
- Write two questions that came to your mind while you were reading.

Reading

Select one book every other week from the list below and answer the following questions.

1. How did the main character make friends?
2. What does the main character learn about getting along with other people?
3. How does the main character handle frustration?
4. How do the characters gain attention?
5. What do the characters learn about taking care of each other?

(Don't forget that animals may be characters.)

Lowry, Lois *Number the Stars*
Fleischman, Sid *The Whipping Boy*
Greene, Bette *Philip Hall Likes Me. I Reckon, Maybe*
Krumgold, Joseph *Onion John*
Lewis, C. S. *The Lion, the Witch and the Wardrobe*
Speare, Elizabeth *Sign of the Beaver*
Voight, Cynthia *Dicey's Song*
Strasser, Todd *The Complete Computer Popularity Program*
Haven, Susan *Maybe I'll Move to Lost and Found*
Sperry, Armstrong *Call It Courage*
Armstrong, William *Sounder*

Math

Every week, plan and prepare at least one supper for your family. Keep track of the cost of the meal, measure the ingredients, and calculate the calories and fat grams. Make a graph of this data. Each category can be a separate graph, or you may include all the categories on one line graph.

Social Studies

Listen to the news or read a newspaper every day. Keep a daily journal of your reactions to the stories you read. Write a letter to the newspaper editorial staff. Purchase or draw a map of the world. Flag the locations of your journal topics by day. What parts of the world interest you most this summer?

Writing

Write your autobiography. Use the five chapter titles from the list below and write a chapter on your life.

My Favorite Animal
My Favorite Movie
How I Made a New Friend This Summer
A Trip to Remember
A Difficult Day

Art

- Illustrate your autobiography.
- Make a collage of your research on science.
- Sketch a picture inspired by your social studies journal.

Music

Make an audio- or videotape recording of sounds and rhythms that remind you of this summer. Ask friends to star on your tape. Narrate the tape.

Have a safe, happy, and successful summer.

Sincerely,

Ms. Pleasant

Happily for everyone, Fred completed his assignments and his father proudly dropped them off at the school regularly. While Fred continued to have difficulties in eighth grade, parents and teachers agreed that he had made significant progress socially and that avoiding the loss of self-esteem associated with retention was beneficial.

Another case for summer non-school can be made when a student has transferred from another school and shows the new school a completely different set of behaviors. In many cases a fresh start, combined with an improved family situation proves to result in marked academic improvement. When second semester grades are miles away from first semester failure, many middle schools see the benefit in opening a path for the student to move to the next grade. While there are certainly two schools of thought on this practice, there is room for reasonable teachers to disagree. Most administrators see value in looking at such cases individually. Such was the case at West Middle School when Brad enrolled in January.

The letter on page 123 was written by a teacher after a discussion with her principal.

Brad had arrived at West Middle School at midterm and after a slow start had risen to the top of every class. He had shown responsibility not only academically, but also in his interest in helping special education students and in general outstanding citizenship. His teachers were shocked when his records arrived from his previous school.

His grades in every subject were terribly low. Report card comments reflected behavior and attitude problems that no one had observed at West. The teachers called Brad's grandmother and learned of a stormy first semester. Brad's mother had died the previous summer, and his father was nowhere to be found. Brad's grandmother had gladly taken responsibility for his care, but after a few weeks, her low income retirement complex insisted that she could no longer live there with a twelve-year-old. Finally, they were evicted.

Several weeks followed of living in homeless shelters, emergency housing, and even a few nights in the car. At last an affordable apartment became available. At the same time, Brad's SSI check came through along with free lunch approval. Things improved dramatically for Brad and his grandmother.

Brad's teachers realized that in spite of his success at West, his first semester grades made passing out of the question. His teachers were afraid that he would never understand why such hard work in the second semester would not pay off. Would his discouragement cause him to revert to his previous failing patterns? Brad's guidance counselor recommended creativity and flexibility. West's principal and teachers agreed to offer an alternative. The guidance counselor had access to community resources and information about camp scholarships. The following letter explains the plan for Brad.

Dear Mrs. Campbell,

Following our conversation yesterday, I am writing to confirm that Brad's grades from the first three grading periods at Powell Middle School have made it impossible for him to pass seventh grade. Having observed Brad, our team agrees that a retention is not in his best interest. We understand that things have settled down for your family, and accordingly, Brad has been able to show us that he is capable and responsible.

We are recommending that Brad be placed in the eighth grade due to extenuating circumstances and that he spend the summer seeking enrichment activities instead of summer school. Museums, public libraries, parks, and colleges are offering a variety of experiences for young students looking to better themselves. In addition, Ms. Kenneth has enclosed a list of classes and camps that offer scholarships.

We sincerely hope that Brad can find good things to do to enjoy a safe and happy summer. Please monitor his progress very closely next year. Ms. Kenneth, Dr. Bell, and our team of teachers stand ready to help you as you encourage Brad in his academic endeavors. Please call us if we can help.

Sincerely,

Max Boxwell

Max Boxwell

Brad applied for a scholarship at a camp where gifted and talented students study environmental impact issues on water quality. He was accepted on the merit of his essay on pond life and enjoyed the experience enormously. The director of the camp related her enjoyment of Brad's love of nature. He applied for a library card and was a common sight at the main branch where he worked as a volunteer assistant. His grandmother was especially proud that their permanent address made the library card possible.

ASSISTING THE STUDENT WHO NEEDS TO BE MOVED TO AN AGE-APPROPRIATE SETTING

Some systems offer a special summer school for students who are more than one year behind in school. These students are at a high risk of dropping out, and the opportunity to progress two years may offer the only hope of completing a high school program. Such was the case for Mandy.

Mandy was two years behind in school, making her two years older than her classmates. Mandy's school system offered a special summer school for students at risk of dropping out. By agreeing to an extra summer school session and longer days in summer school, Mandy would be able to gain a year and leave seventh grade for ninth grade. She knew of the program and frequently pursued the possibility with her teachers. They agreed to recommend her for the program. Below is a letter to her mother that explains the program.

Lincoln Middle School
501 Carter Pike
Big Run, Nebraska 52000

May 10, 1997

Dear Ms. Clancy,

Mandy is extremely interested in attending our special At-Risk Summer School program. We are delighted to recommend her for this opportunity. Successful completion of the class makes a student eligible to attend ninth grade. In order to qualify for the program, she will have to complete the enclosed forms and write an essay explaining her motivation for attending summer school. Please give her any assistance you can in completing the necessary paperwork, but encourage her to express her own ideas. If you have questions about this matter, please call me at 555-8654 or Dr. Booth at 555-8931.

Sincerely,

Valerie Greyson

Valerie Greyson

These types of programs often give at-risk students the motivation they need to complete their education. Placing the students with peers is a powerful strategy in dropout prevention. It increases their self-esteem and creates "positive peer pressure" that encourages them to stay in school with their friends.

ASSISTING THE STUDENT WHO IS LACKING GOOD CLASSROOM BEHAVIOR

Sometimes students exhibit poor classroom behavior because they are not aware of proper etiquette. They may lack an understanding of how their body language, tone of voice, and language affect how others respond to them. It may be helpful to discuss the following list of behavior terms with your class and explain how to behave positively. For example, a student may not realize the impact of maintaining eye contact and keeping a listening posture when he or she listens to others.

Performing the writing assignment helps students think seriously about their classroom behavior. Take care not to use the list as punishment for only those students who are routinely misbehaving. All students can profit from the activity. As with all writing activities, this assignment should reinforce the pleasure of writing in addition to instructing the students. To encourage creativity and positive interaction, allow students to write sentences in cooperative groups on sentence strips and share their creations as tools for classroom discussion.

Behavior Vocabulary

Write a sentence related to behavior in our classroom for each of the following words. Avoid using the names of students in our school.

eye contact	pleasant
listening posture	communication
alert posture	quietness
listening	active listening
gentleness	carefulness
hygiene	gesture
tone of voice	language
touch	order
special needs	etiquette
emergency	hero
preparedness	humor
intelligence	appropriate
creativity	authority

ASSISTING THE STUDENT WHO IS IN TIME-OUT

Placing a student in time-out is a good strategy to utilize in the classroom, yet it can be enhanced with a few simple adjustments. Tell the students that the time-out area is called the Designing Area. The students will be using their time-out periods to design better ways to control their behavior.

It is important that the teacher post the rules for the Designing Area. Below is a sample of basic rules that will assist the student.

The Design Now portion tells the student how to design his or her behavior program.

The Designing Area

Name _____ Date _____

The rules for this designing area are very important and must be followed to the letter.

Remember that your teacher cares about you, but right now he or she must pay attention to other students.

1. Remain seated quietly unless your teacher recognizes you and gives you permission to speak. Even if the class is dismissed, you are to remain seated. You may not sharpen your pencil or ask to go to the restroom. Raise your hand if you have an emergency and wait to be recognized.

2. Use your own paper to complete the design below. Copy the questions and write your answers carefully. You will abide by the design, so make a good one.

Design Now!

1. What did I do?

2. Did I break a rule?

3. What will I do next time?

4. What is a fair consequence if this happens again?

ASSISTING THE STUDENT WHO HAS POOR WORK HABITS

Positive Peer Pressure

Educators are very aware of the power of peer pressure. Why not utilize it to assist struggling students? Getting to class on time, completing homework, staying on task, and staying out of trouble are all tasks that can be targeted for peer assistance. One type of intervention that can be used is Positive Peer Pressure Assessment. To set up this intervention, place the students in groups of four. In each group place students who have a variety of levels of school survival skills. Set aside specific times for the students to talk about their school behaviors. Home room or the last few minutes of class is a good time to permit the groups to assemble. Train the students in the following manner:

- On Monday, assemble in the small group and permit each student to fill out the personal goal section of the Positive Peer Pressure Assessment Form.

- As a group, discuss the goal and how it was determined. Is there a particular area in which a student has difficulty? If so, what are the strategies that other students use to improve in that area? Discuss ways to encourage one another throughout the week.

- Have the groups meet in the middle of the week to determine if the students are on target with their goals. Discuss ways to improve throughout the week.

- On Friday, assemble in the small group and count up the total number of checks. Each student will write a weekly assessment of his or her behaviors. Students will then discuss the results of the assessment. At this point, they will attempt to share strategies that could help students reach their goals the next week.

- After you have had an opportunity to see how the students are progressing with their groups, encourage students to "fine tune" their goals. You can provide a reward for the students who are improving in their school survival skills.

POSITIVE PEER PRESSURE ASSESSMENT

Week Beginning _____

Place a check (✔) in each box to indicate the tasks that you have completed successfully. Each student must set a goal for the number of checks he or she can earn for the week.

Name _____					
	M	T	W	Th	F
Finished homework					
Finished classwork					
Attended and was on time to class					
Had all necessary materials					
Demonstrated good behavior					

My personal goal for the week is _____ checks out of 25.

My total checks were _____ .

Write an assessment of your week.

_____

_____

_____

_____

_____

_____

_____

Name _____					
	M	T	W	Th	F
Finished homework					
Finished classwork					
Attended and was on time to class					
Had all necessary materials					
Demonstrated good behavior					

My personal goal for the week is _____ checks out of 25.

My total checks were _____ .

Write an assessment of your week.

_____

_____

_____

_____

_____

_____

_____

ASSISTING THE STUDENT WHO DOES NOT RESPOND

Nonresponsiveness is a behavior that can surface in the adolescent years. In the classroom this behavior impacts your ability to assess a student's progress. Not responding to people can have numerous causes. One of the easiest causes to remedy is lack of confidence. The following strategy, Answer Cards, involves the entire class. Engaging all students in intervention keeps you from having to single out a particular student. When a student is suffering from a lack of confidence it is not beneficial to call attention to the problem.

How to make Answer Cards:

Materials:

- 4" x 6" unlined index cards (one per student)
- Small red adhesive dots (one per student)
- Small yellow adhesive dots (one per student)
- Small green adhesive dots (one per student)
- Scissors
- Small envelopes (one per student)

Procedure

- Draw two lines that will divide the 4" x 6" card into thirds.
- Place a red dot on one-third of the index card.
- Place a yellow dot on one-third of the index card.
- Place a green dot on one-third of the index card.
- Cut the card into thirds.
- Place one red, one yellow, and one green section in each envelope.

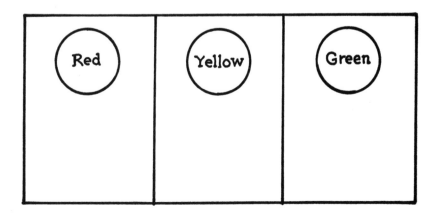

How to Use the Answer Cards

- Distribute an envelope, with the three different colored cards in it, to each student.

- When you reach a point in the lesson that requires a response from the students, ask the students a specific question. The question should be one that must be answered with either a "yes," "no," or "I don't know" response.

- To respond, the students will hold up the appropriate card. A red card represents no, a green card represents yes, and a yellow card represents that the student doesn't know the answer.

- All students must respond to each question with a card. They are to hold the cards in such a way that you can view the cards, but other students cannot see the cards.

- To assist students who lack confidence in responding, you will need to reinforce these students positively. Appropriate actions could include:

  - Establish eye contact with a student who is responding correctly and say, "Good answer."

  - If all students in a particular row are responding correctly and a student who lacks self-confidence is in the row, say, "Everyone in row 2 is correct."

  - If a student shows the correct Answer Card, praise the student and ask the student how he or she knew the correct answer. This approach has little risk for the student. You have already let the student know that he or she is correct. If the student does not want to respond, you can say, "You just knew, didn't you?" Usually you will get at least a head nod from the student.

ASSISTING THE STUDENT WHO IS RUDE

Many times rude students have no idea how they appear to their fellow students. "Don't Go There!" is a creative writing activity that will permit the students to self-assess their behavior.

Don't Go There!

Write run-on sentences describing how not to behave in class. Include things to do and not to do. Trade run-on sentences with a friend. Cut up your friend's paper. Add punctuation and conjunctions, and glue your new sentences on construction paper. Below are some non-suggestions to help you get started.

> If you want to be happy in class remember a few handy tips your teacher will enjoy your participation if you jump up and call out answers immediately you may see others hesitating and raising their hands this just delays class go ahead and joyfully shout Hey I know the answer blurt out the first thing that comes into your head your ideas are very important it isn't good for you to hold them in they can build up in there and cause you to have a headache your teacher would not want you to have this problem so sing out don't hold back keep this up even if your teacher asks you to speak in turn he or she is merely being polite to the other students and secretly wants you to save time by moving class along with your answers other students will also appreciate you for saving them the time and effort of thinking and answering for themselves remember bellow out.

ASSISTING THE STUDENT WHO IS MESSY

There is no reason for a middle school educator to spend one second cleaning up after students. Several strategies are available to you. Listed below are some of the most effective.

- Tell the students that no one will be able to leave the classroom without at least two pieces of trash in their hands. Place a trash can by the door and ask them to line up when they have their "trash." Let the students drop the trash into the can and walk out the door. This is extremely effective if you begin this procedure about two minutes before the bell. The "Early Bird" trash-picker-uppers get to leave early.

- Post the sign below. Discuss the math in the problem and let the students know that "it's only good math to include all students in the clean-up effort!"

DO THE MATH!

If it takes 90 people 1 minute to clean up,

it will take 30 people 3 minutes to clean up,

or

10 people 9 minutes to clean up,

or

5 people 18 minutes to clean up,

or

1 person 90 minutes to clean up.

Which group do you volunteer to join?

ASSISTING THE STUDENT WHO QUESTIONS AUTHORITY

You Make the Call

Being a teacher or a principal is a tough job. Put yourself in the role of authority for the day. Read the situations below and write what decisions you would make to solve the problems.

1. As the principal you are trying to decide what to do with Ronald. He has already been in your office earlier in the week for disturbing Music class. In his hand is the following referral from Ms. Tune, the Science Teacher:

    Ronald is keeping everyone in science class from learning. Today he was talking to William during a quiz, and I asked him to stop. He did not. I moved him to the front of the room. He then began to talk to himself. He was saying, "I don't care what she says. I can talk when I want to." I cannot conduct class with Ronald in the room. I have already called his mother about his behavior. His mother said she doesn't know what to do with him.

    How are you going to teach Ronald to control his behavior?

    _____

    _____

    _____

2. You are an eighth-grade teacher. Your first period class is being very rude. Yesterday they would not be quiet during the video, they laughed at a student who fell in the room, and two of them smarted off to you when you asked them for their homework. How are you going to keep them from being rude today?

    _____

    _____

    _____

3. As the principal you have to deal with Crystal. The school policy states that when a student is tardy four times in a grading period they are sent to the office. Today she was late to school for the fourth time. She has already been to the office for the same offense last grading period. You discovered that her mother leaves for work about an hour before Crystal leaves for school. What will you do?

    _____

    _____

    _____

4. You are Aaron's teacher. He is bright, and last grading period he earned a 92 in your English class. You have always seen him as a well-behaved student. Lately, he has not been doing his work, has been sleeping in class, and has been acting like he doesn't care. You look at his grade average, and it is a 65. How can you help Aaron?

_____

_____

_____

_____

_____

5. As a teacher on the first floor you are concerned about hall behavior. During class change students are shoving each other, shouting at the top of their lungs, and running. You are afraid that the students will get hurt. What should you do?

_____

_____

_____

_____

6. The lunchroom environment is terrible. Some students are not cleaning the tables after they are finished, and other students are yelling across the room. Yesterday was the final straw. There was a food fight. Two students slipped on the food that was on the floor. You are the principal of the school. What should be done to make the lunchroom a more enjoyable place to eat?

_____

_____

_____

_____

_____

_____

_____ *Positive Classroom Management*

STRATEGIES FOR HELPING STUDENTS WHO MISS ASSIGNMENTS

While You Were Out

Devising a system to assist students with make-up work is difficult. The students either do not ask for their make-up work, or they ask for their work at very inconvenient times. Using a bulletin board as a management system for this task allows you to have a visual prompt to remind students of the importance of completing missing assignments.

Cover the bulletin board with cloth or fadeless bulletin board paper. Using this type of background is important because this board can remain up the entire year. Make a transparency of the sleeping student. Using an overhead, draw the sleeping student on a large sheet of poster board and staple it in place on the board. Construct the heading "While You Were Out" with large letters. Add several Zs to the heading to imply that the student is sleeping. Label file folders to represent each class or class period that is taught. Staple the left, right, and bottom of the folders to the bulletin board. This leaves the top of the folder open.

When a student misses an assignment write the name of the student on the missed assignment. Slip the missed work into the folder. If the assignment was out of the textbook, simply jot down the date and the page numbers on a slip of paper and post the note next to the folder.

Inform students to check the bulletin board when they return after every absence. This system also helps the students accept the responsibility for making up their work. If assignments remain in the folders after the students return, at first prompt the students to come to the bulletin board and pick up their work. To encourage the students not to delay in completing missed work, it may be necessary to state that the assignment will remain in the folder for only two to three days.

ASSISTING THE STUDENT WHO IS A VANDAL

Dear Annie and Arnie,

Vandalism of school materials and equipment is often a big problem in the middle school setting. Some students doodle on desks and books without realizing the value of the materials they are destroying. If the root of the vandalism problem is no deeper than that students lack pride in the school environment or that students have never been accountable for repairing or replacing damaged materials, then the following strategies can remedy vandalism within the school setting:

- Establish a classroom rule that addresses vandalism of classroom property. For example, determine a specific penalty for writing on desks. The consequence for this behavior could be reporting to your classroom and cleaning all the desks after school.

- To discourage writing in textbooks, allow the students to inspect the textbooks at the beginning of the year. On a form, the students will have the opportunity to declare any damage that has occurred to the textbooks prior to their use of the book. These forms will be used when the book is turned in and any damage, beyond the normal wear and tear, will be assessed to the students.

- Establish beautification committees. Each team at the school should have its own beautification subcommittee and representatives from each subcommittee would also be on the schoolwide beautification committee. Be certain to include teachers, parents, and local business leaders on the committee.

- Consider beautification projects, such as installing planters or painting murals. Sponge painting walls is also a good idea. This painting technique works well because it covers "a multitude of sins" and can be touched up easily.

- Remove graffiti promptly.

- As a writing activity assign the students to answer a letter to Annie and Arnie, who are fictional advice columnists. Place the students in pairs of one boy (Arnie) and one girl (Annie). Ask each pair to work together to respond to the letter found on page 137.

- The Annie and Arnie format can be used to address other behavior problems found at the school. A sample form on page 138 can be used to allow students to write to Annie and Arnie. Different students may be selected to assume the roles of Annie and Arnie for the week.

Dear Annie and Arnie,

I think my school is about the ugliest place in the whole world. The building isn't all that bad, but the students just don't care what it looks like. After class there is paper all over the hallways, and the lockers are no more than trash cans.

As I was leaving science class today, I turned around and looked at the room as we all walked out. It was a disaster! Some of the kids have been writing on their desks. There were candy wrappers on the floor and homework papers scattered about. It's hard to care for the classroom when nobody else seems to care.

Don't let me forget to tell you about the cafeteria. Gross! Yesterday I couldn't even find a clean place to eat my lunch. You have to wonder if some kids were raised by wolves. They left food everywhere.

What can I do to make my school cleaner? I'm just one kid, but I hate this messy building.

Sick of trash,

I Care Karry

_____

_____

_____

_____

_____

_____

_____

Dear Annie and Arnie,

_____
_____
_____
_____
_____
_____
_____
_____
_____
_____
_____
_____
_____
_____
_____
_____
_____
_____
_____
_____
_____
_____
_____

Special Situations
in the Classroom

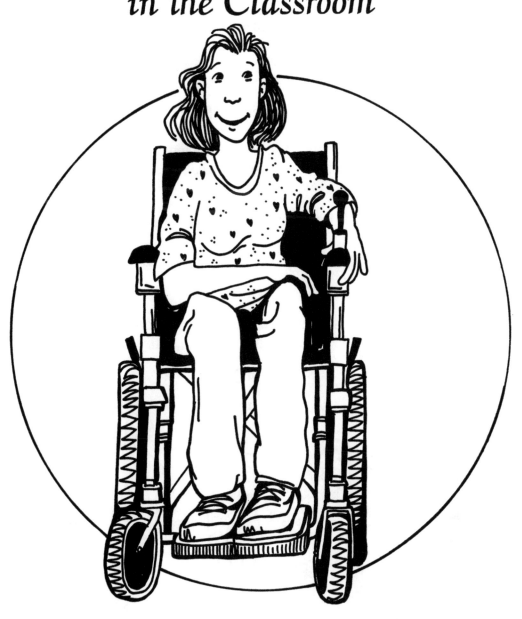

REASONABLE MODIFICATIONS

The practice of inclusion has created a great deal of debate between special educators and regular educators. When a special education student is placed in a mainstream classroom, who is responsible for the accommodations that will be required to serve this student effectively?

Regular teachers want special education consultants to remember that they already have 25–35 students per class to serve. A majority of the regular education students need special modifications and the regular educator is already "dancing as fast as he or she can" to meet the needs of those students.

Special education teachers realize that many times handicapped students are more likely to succeed in the mainstream if the teacher has skills that will permit accommodation in the regular classroom. They also feel a responsibility to educate the student in the "least restrictive environment."

Both sides have important points. It is a waste of time for either side to argue who is working the hardest or who has the interest of the student at heart. Both sides are overworked. In attempting to get at some type of compromise about the interest of the student, it is best to begin with the assumption that both sides care deeply about their students and the school program.

To determine what are "reasonable accommodations" for the regular educator three questions can be used.
- How much extra time is required?
- What will have to be done differently?
- How much will it cost?

The form on page 142 can serve as a guide when regular educators and special educators are looking at reasonable accommodations. Using this form will clarify roles and assign responsibilities.

What modifications are reasonable to expect from the regular classroom educator?

Listed below are suggested accommodations that are reasonable in the regular classroom setting.

Physical Layout of the Classroom

1. Place the student in a specific seat in the room.
2. Place the student away from distractions. (For example the student could be seated away from the air conditioner.)
3. Allow the student to sit at a table that is wheelchair accessible.

Instructional Materials

1. Enlarge worksheets on a copier. (A student could handle this task.)
2. Divide a worksheet into sections.
3. Color code worksheets to assist in emphasizing various aspects of the assignment.
4. Provide written instruction for class assignments.
5. Remove distracting pictures from worksheets.
6. Write directions in brief steps.
7. Allow students to use a calculator or a dictionary.
8. Permit students to do assignments with a computer or audio visual equipment.
9. Tape visual prompts to the student's desk (for example, tape the cursive letters of the alphabet to the desk).
10. Allow the student to tape record the class.
11. Provide samples of assigned projects.
12. Shorten assignments.
13. Allow more time to complete assignments.
14. Allow the student to use pictures and diagrams in place of written work.
15. Permit the student to take tests orally.

Human Resources

1. Allow a student to correct his or her notes by using another student's notes.
2. Pair students together to assist one another.
3. Allow a student to use carbon paper in order to take notes for another student.
4. Permit a student to read assigned questions to the specially challenged student.

REASONABLE ACCOMMODATIONS PLANNING GUIDE

Suggested Accommodation	How much extra time will it require?				What will have to be done differently, and who will do it? (parent, sp. teacher, reg. teacher, student)	What is the cost? Who will pay for it?
	Reg. ED	Sp. ED	Parent	Student		

Positive Classroom Management

EVALUATION MODIFICATIONS

You will want to use creativity and flexibility in the evaluation of students with special needs. Grades must be authentic representations of a student's progress. A report card must reflect the growth, effort, and knowledge of the student. You will want to teach self-evaluation skills to all students, but these are especially important for students with special needs. It is completely appropriate to remark on the report card that grades have been modified due to special education, the 504 regulation, or the special needs of the student, such as grief or illness. You may include the checklist below to describe methods used to modify the grades.

Dear Parents,

Your child's grade has been modified due to _____

_____ .

Modifications are used to permit an authentic assessment of the student's growth without penalizing him or her for special needs. Please return your suggestions for further modifications with this report of progress.

Sincerely,

_____

✔ *Check modifications that you think would assist your child.*

☐ Self-evaluation
☐ Student completes the assignment and circles the items he or she feels confident about. Circled items are graded.
☐ Student completes the assignment and circles the items he or she feels confident about. All items are counted and circled items are counted double.
☐ Assignments are abbreviated.
☐ Student makes presentations in preferred learning style.
☐ Cues and visual prompts are used.
☐ Daily grades are heavily weighted.
☐ Special projects are heavily weighted.
☐ Self-assessment is heavily weighted.
☐ Homework is discounted by_____ %.
☐ Cooperative learning is used.
☐ Peer tutoring is used.
☐ Student is given credit for working examples and for checking answers in the back of the book.
☐ Student dictates answers to the teacher or another student.
☐ Student uses notes during test.